Auto Upkeep

Basic Car Care

First Edition

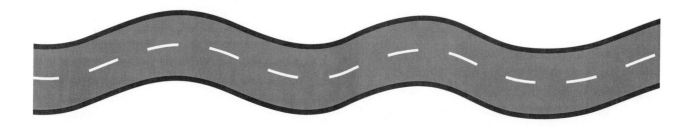

Michael E. Gray

Rolling Hills Publishing

New Windsor, MD

www.rollinghillspublishing.com

New Windsor, MD

Auto Upkeep: Basic Car Care
First Edition
Michael E. Gray

Editor-in-Chief, Illustrator, Project Manager: Linda E. M. Gray
Contributing Proofreader: Kyle Johnson

ISBN 0-9740792-0-0
Library of Congress Control Number: 2003092616

Printed in the United States of America
First printing: July 2003
10 9 8 7 6 5 4 3

For more information or comments about the book contact:
Rolling Hills Publishing
PO Box 724
New Windsor, MD 21776

Email: info@rollinghillspublishing.com
Rolling Hills Publishing is also online at www.rollinghillspublishing.com

NOTICE TO THE READER
The publisher, author, www.rollinghillspublishing.com, and those associated with the text do not warrant or guarantee any procedure, process, or products presented in the text, CD, or on the website. Due to the vast number of automotive manufacturers and related products, the reader should follow all procedures provided with the vehicle or by the product manufacturer. The reader assumes all risks while following activity procedures, is warned to follow all safety guidelines, and should avoid all potentially hazardous situations. The publisher, author, www.rollinghillspublishing.com, and associates shall not be liable for damages to vehicles, their components, or injuries to individuals using or relying on this material. The publisher, author, www.rollinghillspublishing.com, and associates do not endorse any particular product, company, or website presented in the text or on the CD.

Table of Contents

Preface

Introduction

Auto Upkeep: Basic Car Care is an introductory book that is intended to provide individuals with the knowledge to make economical decisions and take preventative measures to enhance the overall satisfaction of being an automotive consumer. *Auto Upkeep* text and accompanying CD provide the fundamental knowledge and experience in owning and maintaining the automobile.

Features of the Text

Each chapter includes an introduction, objectives, chapter content, and summary. Chapters also include helpful guides regarding servicing, tech tips, troubleshooting, average prices of replacement parts, and web links.

Features of the CD

The accompanying CD includes text study questions and activity procedures to assist instructors. To simplify opening and compatibility among operating system platforms, documents on the CD are saved as pdf (portable document format) files. This format can be opened using Adobe Acrobat Reader. If you do not have Acrobat Reader already on your computer, you can download it free from www.adobe.com.

On the Internet

Auto Upkeep can also be experienced online at www.rollinghillspublishing.com. This website provides answers to commonly asked questions, links to industries, educational institutions, and individuals teaching basic automotive programs. It serves as an additional resource for you to communicate to people within the automotive field or purchase automotive supplies. Since the website is continually updated with new links, keep checking www.rollinghillspublishing.com for additional automotive resources and new publications.

Acknowledgments

The idea for this text came from my student teaching experience. During that experience I worked under a talented and enthusiastic veteran teacher, Tim Goodner. Tim taught a class called *Car Upkeep*. Immediately I was impressed with the course. This wasn't another course just for future auto technicians, but a course for the average automotive consumer. This student teaching experience inspired me to implement a similar program during my first teaching assignment. In the first year that the course was offered, it became one of the most popular elective courses at the school.

I would like to thank my former teachers at Falls High School; my professors at St. Cloud State University and Illinois State University; my colleagues at East Richland High School, New Windsor Middle School, and the Center for Mathematics, Science and Technology; and Andy's Towing.

A special thanks to Linda, Tim, Sam, Jon, Curt, Galen, Norm, Kyle, Mr. Hilke, Mr. Schmidt, Mr. Fraik, and my friends and colleagues for inspiring me.

And to my parents and siblings...thank you.

About the Author

Mike has always been interested in the automobile. He started in the automotive field at the age of twelve in his family's service station. Since then he has worked in automotive parts supply stores, towing companies, and service facilities. Mike and his wife Linda also owned and operated an automotive service and towing company. For the first three years after obtaining his undergraduate degree in technology education from St. Cloud State University, he implemented and taught a basic high school automotive program. As a curriculum specialist, Mike co-authored ten integrated mathematics, science, and technology books designed for team teaching at the middle school level. After receiving his Master's Degree from Illinois State University, he returned to his passion of teaching. He also continues to be a curriculum specialist consultant in the field of technology education.

Dedication

This book is dedicated to my partner in life, Linda, who has given me complete support and guidance in my career and in the writing of this text. Linda made *Auto Upkeep: Basic Car Care* possible by being Editor-in-Chief, Illustrator, and Project Manager.

CHAPTER 1

Introduction to the Automobile

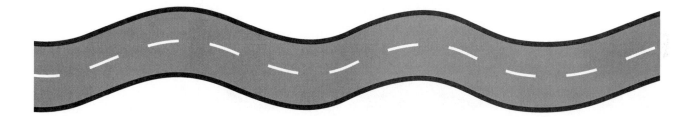

Contents

Introduction

For hundreds of years people have been compelled to find a better way to travel. It would be impossible to credit just one person for the development of the automobile. The word "automobile" literally means self-moving. People wanted a vehicle that could take them to new places. For many years people worked and lived within miles of where they were born and where they eventually died. Before the automobile, most people traveled on land from one place to another by foot, train, bicycle, or horse and carriage (*Figure 1.1*). Within a few years of the turn of the 20th century, the automobile would change society forever. Today, there are millions of vehicles on the roadways.

Figure 1.1   **Horse and Carriage**
Library of Congress
Prints & Photographs Division
Reproduction number, LC-USZ62-55087

Objectives

Upon completion of this chapter and activities on the CD, you should be able to:
- Identify people that have impacted the development of the automobile.
- Identify the progression of the automobile.
- Differentiate between vehicle manufacturers, makes, models, and types.
- Describe and discuss future vehicle designs and features.

Major Automotive Contributors

One of the earliest recorded major milestones in the development of the automobile was the Cugnot steam traction engine in 1770. Even though this self-powered road vehicle was rather impractical, it was a starting point for the self-moving vehicle. The development of the internal combustion engine in 1860 made road vehicles more promising. Then in 1886 Carl Benz was credited with building the world's first practical motorcar. At the turn of the century, blacksmith shops around the country were hand-building cars. Henry Ford, who introduced the Model T in 1908, put an end to many of the small hand-building automotive shops. The Model T was mass-produced, cutting the production time for a car down to minutes. By 1920, half the cars in the world were Model T Fords. In 1923 alone, Ford produced over 1.8 million Model T's (*Figure 1.2*). Ford eventually built over 15 million Model T's. The last Ford Model T rolled off of the assembly line in 1927. Ford produced millions of Model T's, but not enough for it to become the most popular car in history. It was Dr. Ferdinand Porsche who invented the most popular vehicle in history – the Volkswagen Beetle. Over 20 million Beetles have been sold. Introduced in the 1930s, the Beetle is still a popular vehicle today. Over the last hundred years, automobile production has grown substantially. In 1900 about 9500 motor vehicles were produced in the world. That number grew to over 50 million per year just a century later.

Figure 1.2   **Model T**
Courtesy of Taylor Virdell, Llano, TX

Automotive Milestones

Automobiles have gone through a large number of changes since Carl Benz's 1886 Motorcar. Numerous milestones have made vehicles more efficient, comfortable, and reliable. The following is a list of significant automotive events.

1770	Nicholas Cugnot built the Cugnot steam traction engine.
1876	Nicholas Otto patented the four-stroke engine.
1886	Carl Benz patented the world's first practical motorcar.
1886	Daimler Benz Company was formed.
1895	The word "automobile" was coined.
1897	Automotive insurance was introduced.
1902	American Automobile Association (AAA) was formed.
1903	Ford Motor Company was formed.
1908	First Model T was introduced and sold for $850.
1911	Chevrolet Motor Company was organized.
1911	Self starter was invented.
1914	Cleveland, Ohio became the first city to have traffic lights.
1914	Henry Ford raised the minimum daily wage from $2.30 to $5.00.
1916	Brake lights were installed.
1917	The all-steel wheel was developed.
1918	Chevrolet joined General Motors.
1928	Chrysler took over Dodge.
1939	Air conditioning was offered by Nash Motor Company.
1940	Sealed beam headlights were introduced.
1948	Honda Motor Company was formed with $3,300.
1951	Power steering was installed in cars.
1953	Michelin marketed the first radial ply tire.
1954	Fuel injection was used on Mercedes-Benz 300SL.
1965	Motor Vehicle Air Pollution Act was passed.
1973	Arab oil producers imposed ban on exports of oil to U.S.
1986	Centennial of the automobile.
1998	Daimler-Chrysler was formed.
2001	Hybrid gasoline-electric vehicles were mass produced.

Vehicle Identification

Vehicles can be identified by the:
- VIN
- Manufacturer
- Make
- Model
- Year
- Type

VIN

The Vehicle Identification Number (VIN) is an important number on a vehicle. This 17-character number is located on the left side of the dash. Left and right sides are determined by sitting inside the vehicle facing forward. You can see this number as you look in through the windshield from outside the vehicle. This number also appears on the vehicle certification label on the inside of the driver's doorjamb (*Figure 1.3*) and also on the vehicle's title card. The VIN contains information specific to that vehicle. Automotive parts stores may use this number to find the correct replacement parts for a vehicle.

Figure 1.3   *VIN Number*

Figure 1.4   *Examples of Company Logos*

Manufacturer

An automotive manufacturer is a company that produces vehicles. Example names of automotive manufacturers include BMW, Ford Motor Company, General Motors, Daimler-Chrysler, Honda, Isuzu, Saturn, Toyota, and KIA, among others (*Figure 1.4*).

Make

Ford Motor Company manufactures Lincoln, Mercury, and Ford automobiles. These are makes of Ford Motor Company. General Motors manufactures Pontiac, Oldsmobile, Buick, Cadillac, Hummer, and Chevrolet automobiles. These are makes of General Motors. Daimler-Chrysler manufactures Dodge, Plymouth, Jeep, and Chrysler automobiles. These are makes of Daimler-Chrysler.

Model

The model of a vehicle refers to the specific type of make. For example, Aztec is a model of a Pontiac. Taurus is a model of Ford. Intrepid is a model of Dodge. Civic is a model of Honda.

Year

The model year of the vehicle is not necessarily the year in which it was built. A vehicle built in October 2003 most likely would be considered a 2004 model year vehicle. To find the actual model year of the vehicle look at the EPA sticker under the hood. This sticker indicates the year of pollution standards conformance, which is also the model year of the vehicle. The date of manufacture is listed inside the driver's door, on the vehicle certification label. This is the actual month and year that the vehicle rolled off the assembly line. It is usually true that if a vehicle was manufactured after July it is considered the next model year.

Type

Several different types of vehicles are designed to meet consumer demands. Examples include: pickups (e.g., Ford F-Series, Chevrolet Silverado, GMC Sierra, Toyota Tundra, Nissan Titan),

✓ Tech Tip

Date of Manufacture

The date of manufacture and the model year of a vehicle may differ. Manufacturers produce millions of vehicles each year by continuous manufacturing. Vehicle assembly lines rarely shut down. Next year's models often appear on showroom floors in late summer or early fall.

sport utility vehicles (e.g., Ford Explorer, Dodge Durango, Mitsubishi Montero, Oldsmobile Bravada), sport utility trucks (e.g., Chevy Avalanche, Explorer Sport), compact cars (e.g., Honda Civic, Ford Escort ZX2, Geo Metro), mid-size cars (e.g., Ford Taurus, Honda Accord, Toyota Camry), full-size cars (e.g., Mercury Grand Marquis, Ford Crown Victoria, Chevrolet Caprice), mini-vans (e.g., Dodge Caravan, Chrysler Voyager, Ford Windstar, Honda Odyssey, Chevrolet Venture), full-size vans (e.g., Ford E-Series, Chevrolet Express, GMC Savana, Dodge Ram Wagon), and sports cars (e.g., Chevrolet Corvette, Dodge Viper, Porsche 911).

Engine Size and Configuration

The size of the engine is the combined volume of the cylinders. Engine size can be found on the EPA sticker under the hood. Engine size is commonly listed in liters or cubic inches.

Web Links

Automotive Manufacturers

Ford Motor Company
↳ www.ford.com
General Motors
↳ www.gm.com
Honda Motor Company
↳ www.honda.com
Isuzu Motors
↳ www.isuzu.com
Daimler-Chrysler
↳ www.daimlerchrysler.com
Toyota Motor Corporation
↳ www.toyota.com
Mitsubishi Motors
↳ www.mitsubishi.com
Hyundai Motor Company
↳ www.hyundai-motor.com
Kia Motors America, Inc.
↳ www.kia.com

Common liter sizes include 2.2L, 2.5L, 3.0L, 3.8L, 5.0L, 5.7L, 6.0L, 8.0L, etc. Common cubic inch sizes include 302, 350, 360, etc. The only difference is that one is given in U.S. customary units (cubic inches) and the other in the metric system (liters). Engine configuration is the design of the engine block. Common engine configurations include inline, opposed, slant, or "V" (*Figure 1.5*). The configuration describes the way cylinders are arranged in the block. The number of cylinders within the engine block is also used to identify the type of engine design. Engines have 3, 4, 5, 6, 8, 10, or 12 cylinders. The most common engine configurations are inline 4s, V6s, or V8s.

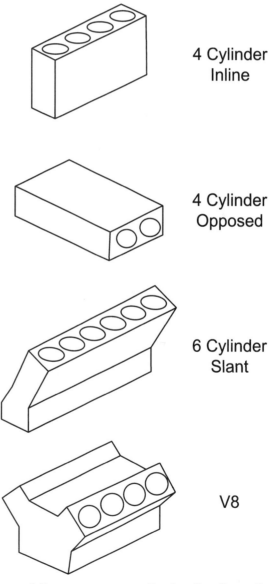

4 Cylinder Inline

4 Cylinder Opposed

6 Cylinder Slant

V8

Figure 1.5   **Engine Configurations**

✓ Tech Tip

Identifying Vehicle Parts

To purchase the correct maintenance items (e.g., filters) or replacement parts (e.g., alternators, starters, spark plugs, etc.), it is important to know the vehicle's VIN, make, model, engine size/configuration, and model year.

The Future

Automobiles of the future will be faster, sleeker, have more features, and be more energy efficient. Future automobiles may be powered by the sun (e.g., photovoltaic solar cells), hydrogen (e.g., hydrogen-powered fuel cells), or have multiple fuel source combinations (e.g., hybrid electric vehicles). When gas prices at the pump approached $2.00 a gallon in 2000 and again in 2003 during the beginning days of Operation Iraqi Freedom, many consumers began seeking energy efficient automobiles. At the turn of the millennium, Toyota and Honda (*Figure 1.6*) started mass-producing hybrid electric (i.e., gas and electric) vehicles that reached approximately 50+ miles per gallon (MPG). The depletion of fossil fuels may have a great impact on future vehicle design.

Figure 1.6   *2003 Honda Civic Hybrid*

Summary

Since the beginning of the modern era, people have been eager to explore new and exciting places. The automobile has made personal land transportation possible. Automobiles allow people to work many miles from where they live, sometimes commuting hours each way. Cugnot, Benz, Ford, and Porsche, among others, changed the development of automobiles forever. In a little over one hundred years, automobiles have become common to almost every household in the United States. With an ever-increasing number of vehicles on the road and demand for oil increasing, fossil fuel prices will certainly increase. Even today, manufacturers are beginning to produce hybrid electric vehicles and are experimenting with hydrogen-powered fuel cells that may eventually diminish our reliance on fossil fuels.

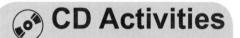

CD Activities

Introduction To The Automobile

- Car Identification Activity
- Chapter 1 Study Questions

CHAPTER 2

Buying an Automobile

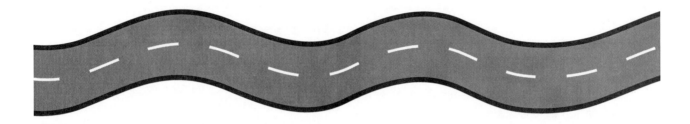

Contents

Introduction

Second to a home, the purchase of an automobile will probably be your next largest financial investment. The car buying process is amazing; you can walk into a car dealership (*Figure 2.1*) and often within an hour drive away in an automobile. The first thing you should do when buying a car is take your time. Remember, the new pretty red car that you just have to have will be there next week (or dealers can often get another just like it). Since most people will usually buy a used car the first time, this chapter will present the process of buying a used as well as a new automobile.

Objectives

Upon completion of this chapter and activities on the CD, you should be able to:

- Differentiate between your needs and wants in relation to good transportation.
- Determine a budget that you can spend on an automobile.
- Identify the steps of purchasing an automobile.
- Identify the places to buy an automobile.

✓ **Tech Tip**

Do Not Get in Over Your Head

Know your financial ability and security. If you cannot put down at least 20% of the total cost, you probably cannot afford the car. Sit down and figure out all of the expenses that go into owning a car: sales tax, maintenance expenses, insurance, licenses, unexpected repairs, fuel, etc.

Purpose of Buying an Automobile

Why do you need an automobile? This is an easy question to answer, right? You need to be able to get from place to place. Now think again. Do you need this vehicle to get to work? Do you need it for cruising on Saturday night? Automobiles are extremely expensive to own and operate. Do you need a car or do you want one? Either way, you will probably own one someday. If you do decide to be in the minority and use mass transit (e.g., bus or train) you will be saving money and natural resources (using mass transit is much more environmentally friendly). However, the reality

Figure 2.1   *Car Dealership*

is that most families in the United States travel by car. Maybe once gasoline becomes extremely expensive more people will start to use mass transit. Until then, most people will probably own an automobile in the United States.

Buying Steps

Several steps are involved in buying a car. Since buying a car is a large financial decision, it is recommended that you visit your local library or surf the Internet to read more about the process of buying a car. This section will briefly describe some of the common steps such as:

- Determining Your Budget
- Identifying Your Wants and Needs
- Financing the Purchase
- Identifying Places to Purchase a Car
- Understanding Car Dealerships
- Completing Comparables

Determining Your Budget

The first thing you should do before buying a car is determine your budget. Can you really afford to buy a car? Your budget will ultimately determine the type of car that you can afford. Your choices may be limited if you just turned sweet-16, have $500 in the bank, and work earning minimum wage. For example, working 20 hours a week making $6.00 an hour will yield you a gross income (before taxes and social security withholdings) of $120 a week/$480 a month/$5,760 a year. Do you want to work one year of your life just to own a car? Many people do. If you had the previous scenario and bought a $6,000 car and spread the cost out over 3 years (36 months) at an interest rate of 9.9%, your monthly payment would be $194. This means you would actually end up paying $6,984 for that car after interest charges (and that doesn't include taxes, licenses, insurance, maintenance, or fuel). The first thing you should do is determine your budget. This is restated because it is extremely important to know what you can afford. Chapter 3, *Automotive Expenses*, will detail the total financial cost of owning and maintaining a car.

Figure 2.2   *Chevrolet Corvette*

Identifying Your Wants and Needs

Getting wants and needs confused is easy. Why else would people be driving around Chevrolet Corvettes (*Figure 2.2*), Dodge Vipers, and Hummers? Sure, they provide reliable transportation, but at what cost? No offense to anyone…most of us would have a difficult time turning down riding in a nice sports car or the ultimate SUV. Different types of cars provide for different needs and wants. When deciding on an automobile you have many choices that can fulfill your wants and needs: pickups, sport-utility vehicles, compact cars, mid-size cars, full-size cars, minivans, full-size vans, or sports cars.

Financing the Purchase

If you cannot afford a vehicle outright, you may have to make monthly payments. If this is the case, you should go to several financial institutions to get quotes about financing information and loan qualification. If you do not have any credit or are under 18, you will probably need

✓ Tech Tip

You Should Negotiate the Deal

After completing your research you should have a good idea what the vehicle is worth. Make a reasonable offer and stick to it. Remember there are thousands of dealerships with cars…you are in the driver's seat. If you are making a fair offer, a reasonable dealership will take it. You should also try to get the dealership to throw in some floor mats and a full tank of gas.

▣ Calculations

Interest Rate Calculations

The following calculations are based on a vehicle loan of $6,000 for a duration of 36 months with interest rates from 3.9% up to 15.9%.

Interest Rate	Monthly Payment	Total Cost
3.9%	$177	$6372
7.9%	$188	$6768
11.9%	$200	$7200
15.9%	$211	$7596

If it is necessary for you to take out a loan, finding the lowest possible rate can save you hundreds or even thousands of dollars over the term of the loan.

to have someone cosign the loan with you (that means they are responsible for the loan if you default). If you have had a loan, you should request a personal credit report. A credit report will show your credit history. A bank will check your credit report to quote you an interest rate. Check current interest rates at several banks on automobile loans. Depending on the economy, financial institution, and your credit history,

interest rates commonly range from 3.9 to 15.9%. However, in response to recessions, automotive manufacturers may offer interest free (0.0%) or low (0.9% to 2.9%) interest loans. The interest rate that you ultimately pay makes a big difference on the overall price you pay for your vehicle. For example, on a 36-month $6,000 loan at 3.9% you will pay $6,372 for your vehicle with a monthly payment of $177. However, changing to a 36-month $6,000 loan at 15.9% you will end up paying $7,596 for the same purchase with a monthly payment of $211. Understanding interest rates is a necessity to financial success. Once you have researched and mastered this, you will better understand what you will really be able to afford.

Where to Purchase a Car

Several places exist for you to buy a vehicle. The most common are private-party sellers, used car lots, new car lots, and on the Internet. Some people try to sell their used car themselves – they are called private-party sellers. People sell their car mainly for three reasons: 1) they cannot afford the car anymore; 2) they decide to upgrade to a newer car; or, 3) their car is a "lemon" and they do not want to deal with it anymore. Try to determine why someone is selling their "good" used car. This may save you thousands in future repairs. Private-parties will sell their cars using

Figure 2.3   *Used Car Lot*

the newspaper, automotive publications, signs in the car's windows, or the Internet. A used car lot (*Figure 2.3*) is another place to find a car. There are thousands of used car dealerships all across the nation. When purchasing a vehicle from a used car lot make sure you have done your homework. Determine the car's historical service records and thoroughly check the car over. When in the market for a new car, people will commonly go to a car dealership. New cars offer the satisfaction of a warranty. Another place to buy new or used cars is on the Internet. Hundreds of websites out there offer cars to consumers. If you do not know about the business that you are dealing with, check their record with the Better Business Bureau.

✓ Tech Tip

Take a Road Test

Go on a test drive if you are buying a used or new car. Do not make this trial run short. Go on your normal travel routes and even on some of the bumpy streets. Listen for any noises that may seem suspicious. If a used car is in your future, inspect the vital systems as discussed throughout this text. If you know a reputable technician or have friends that know about cars, take it to them and let them look at it. Inspect and drive a car before you buy, not after.

Understanding Car Dealerships

One thing you should remember when buying a new car is that the manufacturer makes thousands of each model every year. The one on the lot is not the only one out there. When buying a new car, check out the previous model's history. Does the car have records of reliability? Does it receive good consumer remarks? Sometimes buying a car that has just come out with substantial model changes is not a good idea. The "bugs" may not have been worked out. You should also determine what accessories you want on your vehicle. Often dealerships will try to add-on dealer installed items. Most of the time these

✓ Tech Tip

Be Aware of the Add-ons

When buying a new or used car at a dealership, salespeople will try to add on things such as rust proofing, extended warranties, fabric protector, paint sealant, or pin stripping. These are high dollar mark up items for the dealer. If you want these extras, get several price quotes from local reputable businesses. Learn the facts about your standard warranty and determine if you really need these add-ons.

items are overpriced. Check out other accessory service installers in the area if you want such things as bug deflectors or running boards on your new vehicle. If you are handy, buy the accessories and install them yourself. Another thing you should be aware of is the difference between the Manufacturer's Suggested Retail Price (MSRP), dealer invoice, and dealer cost. The MSRP is commonly called the sticker price. Few automotive models sell at MSRP. In the past, dealer invoice was the price car dealerships paid for their vehicles. But today, most dealerships receive factory to dealer incentives and factory holdbacks. The dealer invoice price is helpful and is relatively easy to get your hands on. Magazines, books, and Internet sites have dealer invoice prices. Dealer cost is the amount that the dealer will actually pay for the vehicle after holdbacks and incentives. Commonly 2-3%

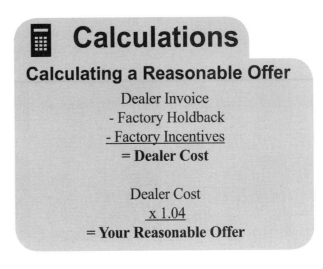

🖩 **Calculations**

Calculating a Reasonable Offer

Dealer Invoice
- Factory Holdback
- Factory Incentives
= Dealer Cost

Dealer Cost
x 1.04
= Your Reasonable Offer

(an average factory holdback) can be estimated off the dealer invoice to establish the dealer's actual cost. For example, a car may have an MSRP sticker price of $34,000, a dealer invoice of $30,000, and a dealer cost of $29,100. What you want to determine is how much you want the dealership to profit from your purchase. You should end up paying from $250 below dealer invoice to $500 above dealer invoice depending upon the model. If you can determine the actual dealer cost (Dealer Cost = Dealer Invoice – Factory Holdback – Factory Incentives) it is reasonable and fair to offer 4% more than dealer cost. Using the previous example, your reasonable offer for that vehicle would be $30,264. This is $3,736 off sticker. However, most dealerships would be happy with that deal. Being educated about the dealer's cost will give you an edge in negotiating a deal. Negotiate up from the dealer cost, not down from the MSRP. Remember you have the advantage. There are thousands of the same car at other dealerships and someone will sell you the car you want at a reasonable price.

Completing Comparables

You should complete comparables whether you are trying to sell your car on your own or trying to figure out if the car you are looking at is a good deal. Many publications are available in book form or on the Internet. Some examples include: *Kelley Blue Book*, *NADA*, and *Edmunds*. You can also look at other individuals trying to sell a car similar to yours. However, you do need to be reasonable. Just because your neighbor sold her car for $1000 more than you are asking, it may be due to several factors such as paint quality, interior condition, or mileage on the vehicle.

Summary

Automobiles are becoming more and more expensive each year. Knowing your budget, identifying your wants and needs, identifying ways to finance the deal, and identifying the abundant places to purchase a car will give you a step up. Remember that this is a large financial purchase – take your time, complete research, and be educated about the car buying process.

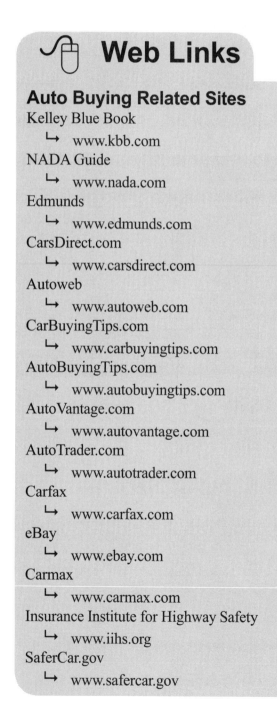

Web Links

Auto Buying Related Sites
Kelley Blue Book
↳ www.kbb.com
NADA Guide
↳ www.nada.com
Edmunds
↳ www.edmunds.com
CarsDirect.com
↳ www.carsdirect.com
Autoweb
↳ www.autoweb.com
CarBuyingTips.com
↳ www.carbuyingtips.com
AutoBuyingTips.com
↳ www.autobuyingtips.com
AutoVantage.com
↳ www.autovantage.com
AutoTrader.com
↳ www.autotrader.com
Carfax
↳ www.carfax.com
eBay
↳ www.ebay.com
Carmax
↳ www.carmax.com
Insurance Institute for Highway Safety
↳ www.iihs.org
SaferCar.gov
↳ www.safercar.gov

CD Activities

Buying an Automobile
- Buying an Automobile Activity
- Chapter 2 Study Questions

CHAPTER 3

Automotive Expenses

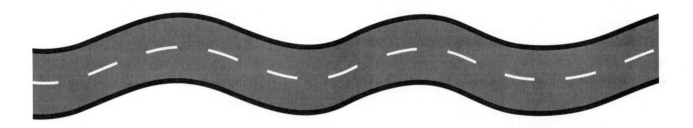

Contents

Introduction

The majority of automotive expenses start after the vehicle purchase. You will need a lot more money than just the car payment to own a car. When determining if you can afford a specific car, take everything into consideration: car payments, insurance, fuel expenses, annual license and registration, routine maintenance, and unexpected repairs (*Figure 3.1*). This chapter will identify and describe the most common expense areas that you will encounter while owning and operating a vehicle.

Figure 3.1   *Unexpected Repair*

Objectives

Upon completion of this chapter and activities on the CD, you should be able to:
- Identify the range of automotive expenses.
- Identify ways to save money.
- Calculate specific automotive expenses.

Purpose of Identifying Automotive Expenses

Before purchasing an automobile it is important to estimate all of the expenses that go along with ownership. Just because you can afford the monthly payment doesn't mean you can afford the vehicle. Sometimes the monthly payment is only half of your total monthly expenses. When

> ### ✓ Tech Tip
>
> **Do the Maintenance When Required**
>
> It is easy to ignore vehicle maintenance if there is no apparent problem. Many owners put off maintenance, resulting in their vehicle leaving them stranded. Skipping oil changes can cause costly engine damage to occur. Not replacing worn or damaged tires can lead to a safety hazard for everyone on the roadway.

determining if you can afford a car, it is critical to look at all facets of car ownership in order to stay financially stable. Many expenses go into owning a car. The following sections will identify and describe some of the common expense areas.

Car Payments

For many car owners the monthly car payment is the majority of their automotive expense. Often people take out a three-, four-, or five-year loan to pay for their vehicle. Remember that this is a long-term commitment between you and the bank. If you lose your job or other family income sources, a monthly car payment could be detrimental to your remaining financial commitments. Your monthly payment is dependent on the amount you financed, duration of loan, and interest rate.

Insurance

Insurance premiums can be a major factor in your automotive decision. Most states require that automobiles be insured. If you have a loan on the vehicle, insurance is mandated by the bank. The bank wants to be fully compensated for the loan if the vehicle is wrecked. Auto insurance protects your vehicle against damage and theft, property damage that may incur, and personal bodily injury expenses. There are many automotive insurance coverage levels that can be purchased. The contract that you decide on is called your insurance policy (*Figure 3.2*). When deciding on an insurance policy, contact different companies for price quotes. Insurance costs depend on your age, driving record, gender, marital status, grades, car model, where you live, and normal driving routes. For beginning drivers, auto insurance is expensive. Speeding, moving violations, and accidents can substantially increase your auto insurance premiums. Some insurance companies offer a lower premium for completion of a specific driver education course, or they give a "good student" discount to individuals that are on the A or B honor roll. Insurance premiums can usually be set up on a monthly, 3-month, 6-month, or yearly billing cycle. Automotive insurance coverage levels include:

- Liability
- Collision and Comprehensive
- Medical Payment, Personal Injury, and No-Fault
- Uninsured and Underinsured Motorist
- Rental, Towing, and Total Replacement Insurance

🖱 Web Links

Insurance Companies

State Farm Insurance
↳ www.statefarm.com
Farmers Insurance Group
↳ www.farmers.com
American Family Insurance
↳ www.amfam.com
Country Companies Insurance
↳ www.countrycompanies.com
Geico Direct
↳ www.geico.com
Progressive Insurance
↳ www.progressive.com
Allstate Insurance Company
↳ www.allstate.com
American Automobile Association
↳ www.aaa.com

✓ Tech Tip

Get Several Insurance Quotes

Do not assume that the first insurance quote is good enough. By obtaining several insurance quotes you may save hundreds of dollars per year.

Liability Insurance

The minimum policy required by most states is liability insurance. Liability insurance covers third party bodily injury or property damage claims that you cause. For instance, if you were in an accident and it was determined to be your fault, your insurance would pay the victim's claims (up to a certain amount). Liability insurance policies are stated in numerical terms such as 20/40/10. The first number indicates that this policy would have $20,000 bodily injury coverage per person. The second number indicates that this policy would have a limit of $40,000 bodily injury coverage per accident. The third number sets the property damage limit at $10,000. A 20/40/10 policy is commonly the minimum required by law in many states, but this amount is usually inadequate considering the cost of medical and legal issues today. For instance, if you did not have enough insurance coverage and you caused a serious accident, a person could sue you and put a lien on your assets. Many insurance companies suggest that people should have 100/300/50 coverage.

Figure 3.2   *Insurance Policy*

Collision and Comprehensive Insurance

In addition to liability coverage, most banks will require that you add collision and comprehensive insurance on your policy. Collision insurance covers the cost to repair your vehicle if you were at fault in an auto accident. Comprehensive insurance covers the costs to repair your vehicle for damage that might occur from things such as natural disasters, vandalism, theft, fire, or hitting an animal on the road.

Medical Payment, Personal Injury, and No-Fault Insurance

Another insurance cost that can be added to a policy is medical payment, personal injury protection, and no-fault insurance. Medical payment insurance covers you and your passengers if you were at fault in an accident. Personal injury protection covers such things as incurred lost wages if you were in an accident and could not work because of it. No-fault protection allows policyholders to submit a claim to their insurance company for reimbursement instead of waiting to see whom the insurance company tries to blame for the accident.

Uninsured and Underinsured Motorist Insurance

Another coverage that is required in many states is uninsured motorist coverage. This covers you if someone without insurance injures you or damages your car in an automobile accident. Underinsured motorist coverage will pay for damages or injuries that occur to you by someone else, if the damages exceed the other party's policy limits.

Rental, Towing, and Total Replacement Insurance

Other features that can be added to insurance policies are rental coverage, towing (*Figure 3.3*), and total replacement coverage. Rental coverage will pay your car rental fees while your vehicle is being repaired. Towing coverage will pay for vehicle towing up to a certain limit, commonly $50. Total replacement coverage will pay the replacement cost of your vehicle if it is totaled (beyond fixing) instead of its depreciated value.

Figure 3.3   *Tow Truck*

Fuel Expenses

Recently, fuel costs have been rising in the United States. The average price per gallon in the U.S. in May 2001 reached over $1.70 a gallon, with many parts of the country exceeding $2.00 a gallon. During the early stages of Operation Iraqi Freedom in 2003, prices spiked once again. Still, compared to many other countries, gasoline in the United States is relatively inexpensive. People in other countries around the world often pay over $4.00 a gallon, making mass transit a more economical and practical means of transportation.

🖩 Calculations

Monthly Fuel Expense

Consider this scenario: If you drive 12,000 miles a year (national average), your vehicle gets 20 miles per gallon (MPG), and gasoline is $1.70 a gallon; you would end up spending $1020.00 a year ($85.00 a month) on fuel. Driving a vehicle with high fuel mileage (e.g., a hybrid vehicle) will lower your monthly expenses.

Fuel economy varies depending on the vehicle you drive. Pickups and sport utility vehicles get 12-20 MPG, compact cars can get 30-40 MPG, and hybrids can get 50-70 MPG. For the most part, gas stations offer very similar fuel prices within the same area for the same grade of fuel. Gasoline prices are set by the price of crude oil, supply and demand, refinery production, octane rating, and specific regional formulation. The price per gallon includes state and federal taxes.

License and Registration

You will be required by law to license and register your vehicle. Costs vary from state to state. When buying a vehicle you also have to pay sales tax and title fees. License plate tags (*Figure 3.4*) need to be periodically renewed.

Figure 3.4   *License Plate with Tags*

Maintenance and Repairs

Car manufacturers are producing more reliable vehicles than ever before. However, no matter how reliable a vehicle is, maintenance is necessary. This section discusses:
• Routine Maintenance
• Unexpected Repairs

Routine Maintenance

Routine maintenance expenses include oil changes, tune-ups, tire replacement, battery replacement, windshield wiper replacement, timing belt replacement, drive belt replacement, and brake service. These services vary in cost depending on the owner's ability and vehicle. If you are able to perform many of these tasks yourself, you can save hundreds of dollars each year. Routine maintenance expenses should be included in your budget. If routine maintenance is ignored, it usually costs more money to fix as an unexpected repair and possible tow.

Unexpected Repairs

New cars commonly come with a standard 3-year/36,000 mile bumper to bumper warranty. However, some manufacturers have longer 7-year/70,000 mile or 10-year/100,000 mile warranties. After the manufacturer warranty expires, repairs will be your responsibility. Unexpected repair expenses include diagnosing engine problems, drivetrain damage (e.g., CV joints, U-joints, transmission repairs), suspension component replacement (e.g., shocks and struts), steering component replacement (e.g., tie rod ends, rack and pinion systems, power steering pumps), alternator replacement, starter replacement, water pump replacement, emergency roadside service, or the worst – internal engine repairs. If your car's warranty has expired, it is always good to have money in reserve to take care of unexpected repairs.

Summary

Automobiles are expensive to own. The financial obligations to own and operate a vehicle range from monthly car payments to insurance premiums to unexpected repairs. Knowing your budget and planning for routine maintenance and unexpected automotive expenses will prepare you for the financial responsibility of vehicle ownership.

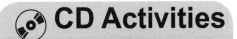

CD Activities

Automotive Expenses
• Automotive Expenses Activity
• Chapter 3 Study Questions

CHAPTER 4

Safety Around the Automobile

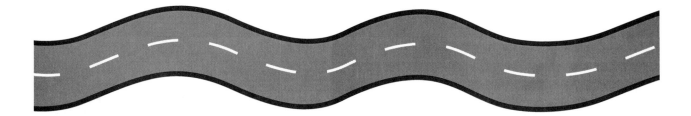

Contents

Introduction

If the correct precautions are not taken, working on automobiles can be dangerous. In a school laboratory, in your garage, or at an automotive repair facility, you need to be aware of people and your surroundings at all times. People are needlessly hurt each year through carelessness. This chapter provides the information necessary to safely work on the automobile. When safety precautions are followed, working on the automobile can be a rewarding experience. Safety glasses (*Figure 4.1*), eyewash stations, first aid kits, and fire extinguishers are some of the items that should be available in an automotive work area.

Figure 4.1   *Safety Glasses*

Objectives

Upon completion of this chapter and activities on the CD, you should be able to:

• Safely work on and around a vehicle.
• Safely jack and support a vehicle.
• Identify basic types of vehicle lifts.
• Safely raise and lower a vehicle on an automotive lift.
• Identify the different types of fire extinguishers.

Laboratory Safety

In a laboratory setting it is important to think **safety**. Vehicles, by their nature, are dangerous. They have moving engine parts; they are heavy; they have explosive fuels; they have high electrical voltages when running; and they often have parts that are too hot to touch.

The following is a list of safety rules for the general vehicle lab. If you are in an educational institution, your instructor may personalize this list to fit your specific situation. If you are working in your own garage, modify the list as you see fit.

1. Safety glasses are not optional. Wear them at all times when working on a vehicle. ***Warning: Ordinary prescription glasses are not safety glasses.***
2. Know the location and operational procedures of using fire extinguishers, first-aid kits, eyewash stations, and a telephone. Dial 911 for emergencies.
3. Do not have bare feet or wear open-toed sandals. Wear shoes that will protect your feet.
4. Loud noises can damage your hearing. Wear ear protection (e.g., earmuffs or earplugs) when loud noises are present (*Figure 4.2*).
5. Someone must be sitting in the driver's seat whenever a car is started and/or running.
6. The exhaust system of a running engine must be connected to a ventilation system if in an enclosed area.
7. Stand creepers up when not in use.
8. Place floor jack handles in the up position when not being used.
9. If a car is off the ground (except when on an automotive lift) it must be supported by jack stands.

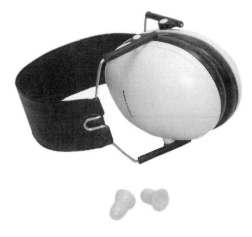

Figure 4.2   *Ear Protection*

10. Keep your tools and hands free of grease and oil. Wearing mechanic gloves is a smart option. ***Warning: Chemicals that get on your skin can be absorbed by your body.***
11. Use the proper tool for each job.
12. Remove rings, watches, and other jewelry so they will not catch on obstructions.
13. If you have long hair, tie it back. It could get caught in moving parts.
14. Do not wear loose or baggy clothing that could get caught in moving parts.
15. Put oily rags in an approved can for combustible materials.
16. Always clean up spilled oil and grease from the floor. Sawdust, kitty litter, or oil dry work well for this.
17. Never pour chemicals, solvents, antifreeze, oil, etc. down the sanitary drain. Put them in their proper containers to be recycled.
18. Do not put tools on top of a vehicle's battery. Accidentally touching both terminals could cause a spark, which could lead to an explosion.
19. Always engage the parking/emergency brake to prevent the vehicle from moving.
20. Do not work on a hot engine. Burns could result.
21. Do not touch spark plug wires while the engine is running. Tens of thousands of volts are present.
22. Never put your hands on or near the cooling fan. Many fans are electric and can start without the key on.
23. Never open a hot radiator cap. Burns could result.

Using Jacks and Jack Stands

You should **never** go under a jacked-up vehicle unless it is supported by jack stands. Jack stands (***Figure 4.3***) are mechanical safety devices used in conjunction with a service jack to support a vehicle. To jack up a vehicle, you should:

1. Position the service jack so that it comes in contact with the frame or another solid chassis component. Do not use the oil pan, body, or other fragile component as lifting

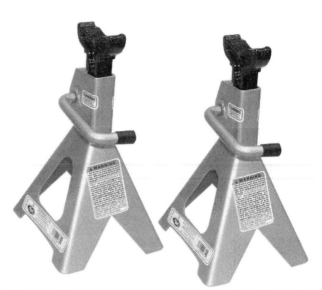

Figure 4.3   *Jack Stands*

points when jacking up the vehicle. Serious damage could result. Check your owner's manual for specific lift points.
2. Chock at least one wheel still on the ground. Wheel chocks (***Figure 4.4***) are used to minimize the risk of the vehicle rolling and falling off the jack.
3. Slowly pump the jack and start lifting the vehicle.
4. Once at the desired height, position the jack stands under the frame or specified jacking points. Ratchet the jack stands to the desired height.
5. Slowly lower the vehicle onto the jack stands and remove the service jack.

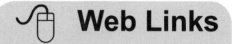

Web Links

Lift and Safety Sites
Conney Safety Products
    ↳ www.conney.com
Automotive Lift Institute
    ↳ www.autolift.org
Rotary Lift
    ↳ www.rotary-lift.com
Hennessy Industries, Inc. (Ammco Lifts)
    ↳ www.hennessy-ind.com
Uvex Safety Products
    ↳ www.uvex.com

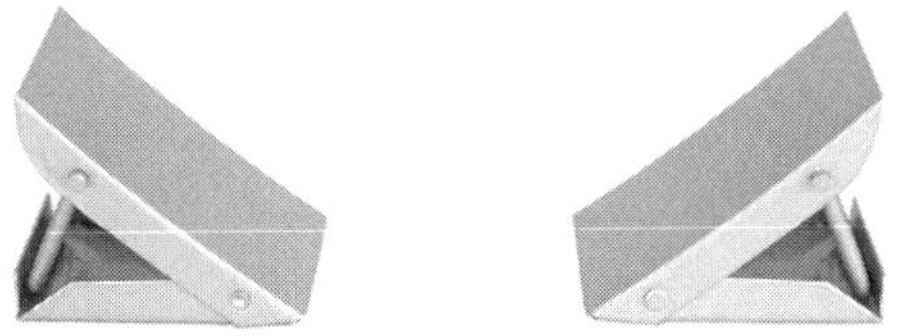

Figure 4.4   *Wheel Chocks*

Warning: Never use concrete blocks or other inadequate devices for supporting a vehicle. Your life is not worth the risk. Safety jack stands are inexpensive and a must when completing repairs or service procedures under a vehicle.

Automotive Lifts

Most repair shops and educational automotive labs have automotive lifts. Automotive lifts are more convenient than using a jack and jack stands. The greatest advantage is that they allow the technician to access the whole underside of the vehicle. The most common types of lifts are surface-mounted lifts. Surface-mounted lifts are bolted to the garage floor and are powered by an electric motor that usually drives a hydraulic pump. The most popular surface-mounted lifts are the:

- Two-column drive through frame engaging lift.
- Four-column drive on lift.

Two-Column

The two-column is often called a two-post lift. Two-post lifts have lift arms that ride up each column. They are synchronized so they go up evenly. This type of lift is commonly used for doing any kind of under-the-car service work. Since the lift contacts the frame, and not the wheels, it is an ideal setup for completing tire rotations, brake inspections, and suspension work. In addition, it is also commonly used for doing undercarriage work on exhaust systems and performing oil changes. By far, the two-post lift is the most popular type of automotive lift.

Four-Column

The four-column is often called a four-post lift. Four-post lifts have runways. Once the vehicle is driven onto the runways, it is lifted by its tires exposing the underside. This type of lift is most common in muffler and oil change shops. It is relatively safe and easy to use. The main disadvantage of this lift is the inability to perform services that require the removal of the tires without adding special adapters. Special adapters, called rolling lift jacks, are available from many manufacturers that can be added to this type of lift to allow the vehicle to be lifted off the runways. These lift jacks allow the removal of the wheels while still on the four-post lift.

✓ Tech Tip

Lifting Points

When vehicles still had full frames, the lifting points were easy - the frame. Today many automobiles do not have full frames, but rather unibodies. The frames on unibody vehicles are integrated with the body. When lifting a vehicle, it is essential that you use the correct lift points. The *Automotive Lift Institute* has up-to-date manuals that specify the lift points for most vehicles.

Lifting a Vehicle Safely

It is imperative to read and review lift safety procedures. If an accident occurs, it could easily be fatal. A person is no match for a 2,000+ pound vehicle. Safely lifting a vehicle requires:

- Reading and understanding safety labels.
- Reading and understanding caution labels.
- Knowing the lift's constraints.
- Knowing lifting procedures.

Safety Labels

Automotive lifts should have safety labels attached to the column that houses the controls for the lift. Some warning labels commonly found on lifts are:

- Clear area if vehicle is in danger of falling.
- Position vehicle with the center of gravity midway on the lift.
- Remain clear of the lift when raising or lowering the vehicle.
- Avoid excessive rocking of the vehicle while on the lift.
- Do not remove heavy vehicle components that may shift the center of gravity.
- Keep feet clear of the lift while lowering.

✓ Tech Tip

Falling Vehicle

Remember that lives are not replaceable, automobiles are. If a vehicle appears to be falling from a lift, clear the area immediately. Do not attempt to save it by pushing it back up. Warn others in the shop. Do not position yourself between a wall and the lift. If the vehicle falls in that direction, you may be severely injured.

Caution Labels

Some caution labels commonly found on lifts are:
- Lift is to be used by trained personnel.
- Use vehicle manufacturer's lift points.
- No one should be in a vehicle that is being raised.

Lift Constraints

Vehicle lifts are designed to only lift vehicles. Never use a lift to remove an engine from a vehicle. Also, never overload the lift. The load capacity of the lift is located on the manufacturer's nameplate.

Lifting Vehicles on Two-Post Lifts

When using a lift have a partner direct you into the lifting area. Line the center of gravity of the vehicle with the posts or as required by the lift manufacturer. On rear-wheel drive cars the center of gravity is usually directly below the driver's seat. However, on front-wheel drive cars, it is usually slightly in front of the driver's seat. Make sure the lift arms are contacting the

vehicle's lift points. Lift the vehicle about a foot off the ground. Then gently push on the front and rear bumper to make sure the vehicle is stable. Visually recheck the lift point connections. Raise the vehicle to the desired height. *Warning: Some two-post lifts have overhead devices.* Do not lift the vehicle so that the roof of the vehicle comes in contact with overhead devices. Before lowering the lift, be sure that everything is removed from under the vehicle. Always refer to the lift manufacturer instructions for specific lifting procedures.

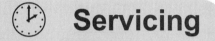 Servicing

Automotive Lifts
- Visually inspect daily
- Perform required maintenance as described in lift manual

Lifting Vehicles on Four-Post Lifts

Drive the vehicle on the runways, centering the weight of the vehicle on the lift. Chock both sides of at least one wheel and apply the parking brake. Raise the vehicle to the desired height. Before lowering the lift, be sure that everything is removed from under the vehicle. Read all manufacturer instructions for specific lift procedures.

💰 Price Guide

A-B-C Fire Extinguisher
↳ $25.00 to $50.00 each
Earmuffs
↳ $10.00 to $20.00 each
Earplugs
↳ $1.00 pair
Hydraulic Jacks
↳ $40.00 to $150.00 each
Safety Glasses
↳ $5.00 to $15.00 each
Safety Jack Stands
↳ $20.00 to $50.00 a pair

Fire Extinguishers

Flammable and combustible materials are present in automotive shops. It is important to know where the fire extinguishers are, how to use them, and what type of fires they put out. For a fire to exist it needs oxygen, heat, and fuel. A fire extinguisher must remove at least one of these components to put a fire out. Fire extinguishers (*Figure 4.5*) are designed to put out specific types of fires. Most automotive shops will have a combination A-B-C fire extinguisher. Fires are classified by the following:

- A-Type
- B-Type
- C-Type
- D-Type

Figure 4.5 *Fire Extinguisher*

A-Type

A-type extinguishers put out wood, paper, cloth, rubber, plastic, and upholstery fires. They do this by coating or lowering the temperature of the burning materials.

B-Type

B-type extinguishers put out gasoline, oil, grease, and paint fires. They do this by smothering the fire. Never put water on a B-type fire. Water will spread the fire.

C-Type

C-type extinguishers put out electrical fires. They do this by using a nonconducting agent.

D-Type

D-type extinguishers put out combustible metal fires. They smother and coat the metal with a special agent to put the fire out.

Summary

Safety in an automotive lab or shop is essential. Following proper service jack procedures enables you to lift a vehicle safely and without damage. Two types of lifts are common in automotive shops: two-post and four-post. The four-post is easier to use than the two-post, but it is not as versatile without special adapters. The four-post lift is generally used for oil changes and undercarriage inspections, while the two-post is commonly used for tire, brake, or suspension work. Fires are classified by the type of material burning. The best type of fire extinguisher to have when working on an automobile is a combination A-B-C.

💿 CD Activities

Automobile Safety
- Automotive Safety Activity
- Chapter 4 Study Questions

CHAPTER 5

Auto Care

Contents

Introduction

Keeping a vehicle clean is as much a psychological thing as it is a physical one. Some people even say that when their vehicle is clean it actually runs better. With today's fast paced society, people sometimes resort to taking their vehicle to an automatic car wash (*Figure 5.1*) instead of washing their vehicle by hand. Detailing a car personally, however, can be very rewarding and can save money. The appearance of the vehicle does not actually change its performance, but it does improve its longevity. A vehicle that is kept clean inside and out will surely render a better value at trade-in-time. This chapter provides the necessary information for cleaning and caring for your automobile.

Figure 5.1   *Automatic Car Wash*

Objectives

Upon completion of this chapter and activities on the CD, you should be able to:
*   Identify different automotive finishes.
*   Explain the importance of washing, drying, and waxing a vehicle.
*   Explain the importance of cleaning the inside.
*   Successfully and correctly clean the inside and outside of a vehicle.

✓ Tech Tip

Car Washes

Over the years there has been a debate over automatic car washes. When automatic car washes first came out, they had rotating brushes. Some people believe that brush car washes grind in dirt, causing scratches in the finish. This may be true depending on how dirty a vehicle is and the quality of the wash equipment. Today the most popular automatic car washes are brushless, using high-pressure nozzles to clean a vehicle. However, this high pressure is hard on a vehicle's finish if the paint is already peeling or flaking. To be on the safe side, wash your vehicle by hand at home or at your local self-serve car wash (*Figure 5.2*).

Automotive Finishes

Up until the 1980s, most vehicles had a basecoat finish. In this type of finish, the color was the topcoat. When waxing, the rag used to wax the vehicle would actually turn the color of the vehicle. The oxidized coat of paint would come off revealing a fresh layer. Since then, finishes have advanced significantly. The finish used on most vehicles today is a clearcoat finish. In this type of finish the color of the vehicle, the basecoat, is coated with a clearcoat. This extra layer adds protection and appearance to the pigmented coat.

Figure 5.2   *Self-Serve Car Wash*

🚑 Trouble Guide

Paint Care and Repair

If paint feels rough, the finish needs to be waxed or buffed. To repair chips, clean the damaged area, touch-up with primer, and then cover with a color matched paint.

When waxing this type of finish, the rag does not turn the pigmented color because it is just removing the oxidized layer on the clearcoat. When choosing a finish cleaner, refer to your owner's manual for suggestions and recommendations.

Washing

The finishes on vehicles have to withstand varying conditions for all seasons of the year. Road dirt, rain, dust, mud, snow, ice, and salt are all harsh on the finish. Keeping the finish clean is the first step in maintaining the vehicle's shine

🖱 Web Links

Automotive Care Sites

Dupont Corporation
  ↳ www.dupont.com

Martin Senour Automotive Finishes
  ↳ www.martinsenour-autopaint.com

Dupli-Color Automotive Paints
  ↳ www.duplicolor.com

Armor All Products
  ↳ www.armorall.com

Mothers Polishes-Waxes-Cleaners
  ↳ www.mothers.com

Turtle Wax Inc.
  ↳ www.turtlewax.com

STP
  ↳ www.stp.com

Nu Finish
  ↳ www.nufinish.com

Figure 5.3   **Car Wash Soap**

and endurance. Not cleaning a vehicle can have adverse effects. If you accidentally brush up against a dirty vehicle you can scratch the finish. When washing, it is not recommended to wash a vehicle while it is hot. Make sure the vehicle is in the shade. In addition, do not use dish detergent. Dish detergents are not chemically designed for vehicle finishes. Dish detergents may strip the wax and dry out the finish. Use only approved car wash soaps (*Figure 5.3*) for cleaning finishes. Car wash soaps are formulated to float away the dirt and grime without harming the vehicle's finish.

🕐 Servicing

Care and Cleaning
- Wash when dirty or every two weeks
- Wax at least twice a year
- Vacuum when dirty or every two weeks

Drying

Water accelerates corrosion. And hard water can leave damaging spots on the vehicle's paint. After washing, dry the vehicle with a towel or a chamois. A chamois (*Figure 5.4*), usually made from sheepskin, is super absorbent. A dry chamois will be hard and abrasive. Before using a chamois, wet it and ring it out. Drag it over the finish to pull off the water. Keep squeezing out excess water. The chamois should stay damp when you are using it.

Figure 5.4   ***Chamois***

Waxing

Waxing adds shine and protection to your vehicle's finish. Wax is to your automotive finish as lotion is to your skin. The sun can dry out the finish on a vehicle. Wax (*Figure 5.5*) coats and "moisturizes" the vehicle's finish, removing oxidation to keep the finish shining. Carnauba, a natural wax, has the tendency to shed water by making it bead and run off a finish. Some synthetic waxes add an extra agent that increases the slickness, shedding water even better. Water contacting these types of finishes will slide off the vehicle. Water and the impurities in water can add to corrosion and wax breakdown. The quicker a vehicle dries, the better. Like washing, you should never apply wax on a hot vehicle or in direct sunlight. Remember to always read the

✓ Tech Tip

Wash Before You Wax

It is extremely important to wash your vehicle before you wax it. If you don't, you may rub the dirt and grime into the paint causing scratches. It is equally important to remember to clean around the doors, trunk, and hood. Do not use a chamois around the doors, trunk, and hood. Use a shop towel that can be cleaned easier. Avoid getting your chamois dirty to prevent scratching your vehicle's finish.

labels on the wax container for specific information. Make sure the wax that you buy is suitable for your car's finish. Some waxes are safe for both basecoat and clearcoat finishes, others are not. Clearcoat type waxes usually have fewer abrasives than basecoat waxes.

Figure 5.5   ***Automotive Wax***

Figure 5.6   **Automotive Vacuum**

Figure 5.7   **Auto Glass Cleaner**

Cleaning the Inside

Vacuuming (*Figure 5.6*) cleans the inside of the vehicle. This includes vacuuming the headliner, seats, carpet, floor mats, and door panels. Dirty fabric will wear out quicker than clean fabric. Dirt accelerates wear by grinding away at the material. Fabric, vinyl, and carpet that is stained or soiled can be cleaned with special fabric cleaners. The most important thing to do safety wise is to wash the windows. Dirty windows can lead to unsafe driving. At night, windows that have a film over them glare. Use an auto-approved glass cleaner (*Figure 5.7*) that resists streaks. Old newspapers or lint free cloths work well for wiping the glass cleaner off the windows. It is also important to protect the vinyl and rubber components. Vinyl and rubber have a tendency to dry out and need to be conditioned. Specially

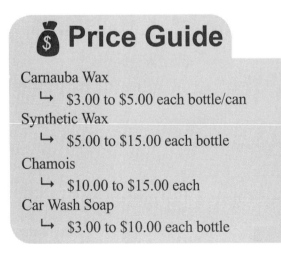

💲 Price Guide

Carnauba Wax
  ↳ $3.00 to $5.00 each bottle/can
Synthetic Wax
  ↳ $5.00 to $15.00 each bottle
Chamois
  ↳ $10.00 to $15.00 each
Car Wash Soap
  ↳ $3.00 to $10.00 each bottle

Figure 5.8   **Interior Cleaner**

formulated interior cleaners (*Figure 5.8*) are safe for most types of vinyl and rubber parts, but always read the manufacturer's labels. Leather should also be cleaned and conditioned with the appropriate product.

Summary

Keeping a vehicle clean is not difficult, it just takes a little time. Washing, waxing, and vacuuming will make your vehicle worth more and make it more appealing to drive and own. Finishes on vehicles have changed over the years from basecoats to basecoat/clearcoats. Clearcoats add a deeper shine and a more durable finish.

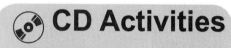

CD Activities

Auto Care

- Interior Cleaning Activity
- Washing Activity
- Waxing Activity
- Chapter 5 Study Questions

CHAPTER 6

Fluid Level Check

Contents

Introduction

Various fluids provide cooling, cleaning, lubricating, and/or sealing to vehicle components. Components of various systems take different types of fluids. The do-it-yourselfer can maintain the different systems by simply checking fluid levels and conditions. This chapter will guide you through correctly checking and adding fluids to vital vehicle components.

Objectives

Upon completion of this chapter and activities on the CD, you should be able to:
- Identify the different types of fluids used in the automobile.
- Analyze fluid conditions.
- Perform basic fluid level checks.

Types of Fluids

It is critical that you check the owner's manual for the correct type of fluid that is recommended for your specific vehicle. The most common fluids that automobile owners need to check are:
- Engine Oil
- Transmission Fluid
- Coolant
- Brake Fluid
- Clutch Fluid (Manual transmissions only)
- Windshield Washer Fluid
- Differential Fluid
- Power Steering Fluid
- Battery Electrolyte

⏱ Servicing

All Fluids
- Check all fluids at oil change intervals
- Check oil level every time you fill your fuel tank

✓ Tech Tip

Types of Fluids

Do not add fluid to a component unless you are sure the fluid meets the specification requirements as stated in the owner's manual. Adding incorrect fluids could void manufacturer's warranties and lead to premature component failures.

Engine Oil

Engine oil (*Figure 6.1*) cools, cleans, lubricates, and seals the internal engine components. Clean engine oil is gold in color, while dirty engine oil is black in color. The most common weight of engine oil is 5W30, but always refer to the your vehicle's recommendations. To get an accurate reading it is best to check the engine oil when the engine is cold. Most automotive engines have an oil capacity between four and five quarts. Vehicle manufacturers suggest adding oil when the engine is low one quart. To check the engine oil, shut off the engine, open the hood, and look for the engine oil dipstick. The engine oil dipstick runs through a metal tube that is usually located on the side of the engine on rear-wheel drive vehicles or on the

Figure 6.1 **Engine Oil**

Power
Steering
Fluid

Coolant

Windshield
Washer
Fluid

Engine Oil

Brake
Fluid

Transmission
Fluid

Battery
Electrolyte

Figure 6.2   *Fluid Locations*

front of the engine on front-wheel drive vehicles (*Figure 6.2*). Refer to your owner's manual if you have questions on the location of the engine oil dipstick. *Note: When checking any fluid, it is important to park on a level surface.* Pull out the dipstick, wipe it off with a shop rag, reinsert it completely into the tube, remove again, and note the reading. The engine oil should be in the safe range (*Figure 6.3*). To add engine oil, locate the oil filler cap (*Figure 6.4*) on the valve cover of the engine. Use a clean funnel to add the correct

🕐 **Servicing**

Engine Oil
* Change engine oil every 3 months, 3,000 miles, or as recommended in the manual by the vehicle manufacturer

amount of engine oil. Give the engine oil time to flow to the oil pan. Recheck the level and correct if necessary. Do not overfill.

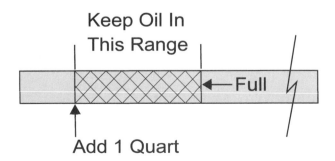

Keep Oil In
This Range

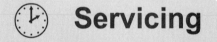 ←Full

Add 1 Quart

Figure 6.3   ***Engine Oil***
                        Dipstick Readings

Figure 6.4   ***Engine Oil Cap***

Transmission Fluid

Both automatic and manual transmissions have fluid to cool, clean, lubricate, and seal internal components. Clean automatic transmission fluid is pinkish-red. The most common type of transmission fluid is Dexron/Mercon®, but always refer to the manufacturer's recommendations. It is usually recommended to check the fluid level in an automatic transmission while it is hot. Drive the vehicle about ten minutes to warm up the transmission. To receive accurate results, most manufacturers recommend that the engine be running and that the gear selector be in park. Apply the parking brake. Locate the automatic transmission oil dipstick. With the engine idling, pull out the dipstick, wipe it off with a shop rag, reinsert it completely into the tube, remove again, and note the reading. The automatic transmission fluid should be between the full cold and the full hot marks (*Figure 6.5*). If low, use a clean funnel to add the necessary fluid by pouring the fluid directly into the tube. Do not overfill. It usually takes only one pint (½ quart) of fluid to bring the fluid level from the full cold to the full hot mark. Recheck the level and add more if necessary. On manual transmissions there is usually a plug on the side of the transmission. To check the fluid level, you must turn the engine off, apply the parking brake, and remove the plug with a wrench. The fluid should be at or near the bottom of the filler plug. Some manual transmissions take ATF (automatic transmission fluid), while others take heavyweight (SAE 80W90) gear oil. Check the owner's manual for specifications. Fill as necessary. Sometimes you need a special adapter that fits on quart bottles to transfer the fluid.

Servicing

Automatic Transmission Fluid (ATF) and Filter

- Change every 2 years, 24,000 miles, or as recommended in the manual by the vehicle manufacturer

Servicing

Manual Transmission Fluid

- Change according to owner's manual

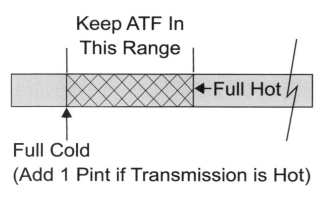

Keep ATF In This Range

Full Hot

Full Cold
(Add 1 Pint if Transmission is Hot)

Figure 6.5   **Automatic Transmission Dipstick Readings**

Coolant

Coolant (antifreeze) comes in various colors: green, orange, red, pink, yellow, and bluish-green. The most common colors are green and orange. The standard antifreeze (*Figure 6.6*) used in vehicles before 1995 was green in color. In 1995, General Motors started using an extended life coolant, called Dex-Cool, in their engines. Dex-Cool, orange in color, was originally manufactured by Havoline for General Motors. Today, several other coolant manufacturers produce extended life coolants. Both standard (green)

Antifreeze/Coolant

Figure 6.6   *Antifreeze/Coolant*

🕐 **Servicing**

Coolant (Antifreeze)

- Change standard (green) antifreeze every 2 years or 24,000 miles
- Change Dex-Cool (extended life) antifreeze every 5 years or 150,000 miles

antifreeze and Dex-Cool (orange) antifreeze are glycol based. The main difference between the two types of antifreeze is in the rust inhibitors and additives. Ethylene glycol, which is used in standard and extended life coolants, is a toxic substance. When checking coolant level, the engine must be cool. First, check the level in the coolant recovery tank (*Figure 6.7*). The recovery tank is usually translucent with a "full cold" and a "full hot" mark. If adding, remove the cap and add a 50% water to 50% antifreeze mixture. Second, check the level in the radiator. This requires removing a cool radiator cap and looking into the radiator. *Warning: Never remove a hot radiator cap – severe burns could result.* The fluid should be at or near the top. Add a 50/50 mixture as needed. Reinstall the cap.

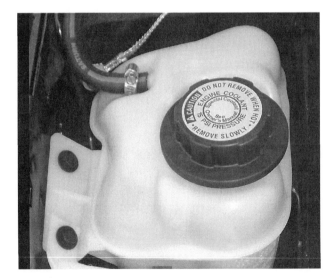

Figure 6.7   *Coolant Recovery Tank*

Figure 6.8   *Brake Fluid*

Brake Fluid

Brake fluid (*Figure 6.8*) provides the transfer of hydraulic pressure to the wheels. Clean brake fluid is clear in color. Use extreme caution when handling. Brake fluid is harmful to your eyes and can damage a vehicle's finish. The most common type of brake fluid is DOT 3, but always refer to your manufacturer's recommendations. The brake master cylinder that houses the fluid is usually mounted on the driver's side firewall in the engine compartment. Most vehicles today have a plastic translucent reservoir (*Figure 6.9*) with a "min" and "max" line. To add brake fluid, park on a level surface, turn the engine off, remove the cap, and add as necessary. When reinstalling the cap, make sure that the rubber gasket seats properly.

Clutch Fluid

Vehicles that have manual transmissions with hydraulic clutches have a clutch master fluid reservoir. It is usually mounted next to the brake master cylinder. Clutch fluid is commonly DOT 3 brake fluid, but always check your owner's manual. To check the clutch fluid, turn the engine off and look through the translucent reservoir. It should be at or near the top. To add clutch fluid, park on a level surface, turn off the engine, remove the cap, and add as necessary. When reinstalling the cap, make sure that the rubber gasket seats properly.

Windshield Washer Fluid

Windshield washer fluid (*Figure 6.10*) is usually blue in color. It is specially formulated so it does not freeze. Never use cooling system antifreeze as it is not made for window cleaning and can damage the vehicle's finish. Do not confuse this reservoir with the overflow antifreeze reservoir – they often look similar. The cap on a windshield

Figure 6.9   *Brake Fluid Reservoir*

Figure 6.10   *Windshield Washer Fluid*

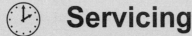

Servicing

Windshield Wipers

- Change once a year or as needed

washer reservoir usually has a wiper symbol engraved on it (*Figure 6.11*). To add windshield washer fluid, locate the cap and fill until the fluid is about half an inch from the top. When adding windshield washer fluid, take a moment to inspect the windshield wipers. The wipers should be soft and without cracks. If the wipers are streaking or skipping across the windshield they need replacing. You can replace just the rubber insert or the complete blade. Follow instructions that come with the replacement parts for specific assembly procedures.

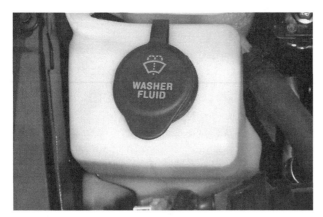

Figure 6.11   *Washer Fluid Reservoir*

Trouble Guide

Leaking Fluids

Most fluids have distinct colors. Use this to your advantage. If you see your vehicle leaving a leak on the ground, note its color, texture, and position under the vehicle. This may lead you to the component that is failing.

Differential Fluid

Rear and front differentials, which connect the drive shafts to the wheels, also require fluid. This fluid check is required on rear-wheel drive or four-wheel drive vehicles, and is similar to checking manual transmission fluid. Remove the check plug, check the level, and fill as necessary. The oil should be at the bottom of the plug hole. Gear oil (SAE 80W90) is the most common differential fluid. Some differentials use limited slip additives. Always check your owner's manual for the specific fluid.

Power Steering Fluid

Most vehicles today have power steering. The power steering pump is located off an engine drive belt. The cap and the dipstick are commonly one unit (*Figure 6.12*). To check the fluid, shut off the engine, locate the power steering reservoir

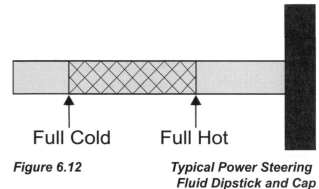

Full Cold   Full Hot

Figure 6.12   *Typical Power Steering Fluid Dipstick and Cap*

Figure 6.13   *Power Steering Cap and Reservoir*

(*Figure 6.13*), remove the dipstick, wipe it off, reinstall, remove again, and note the reading. The stick usually has a full hot and a full cold line. Using a clean funnel, add fluid as necessary. Power steering fluid (*Figure 6.14*) can be clear, gold, or red. Check your owner's manual for specifications.

Figure 6.14   *Power Steering Fluid*

Battery Electrolyte

The electrolyte in a battery is a mixture of sulfuric acid and distilled water. Over time, some of the water may evaporate. To check the level, put on safety goggles and gloves, remove your rings and watches, disconnect the negative battery cable, and remove the cell caps. On some vehicles the batteries are sealed and cannot be opened. Refer to your owner's manual to see if your battery is considered maintenance free. Usually there is a split ring indicator in each cell to indicate the correct levels. If the fluid is low, add only distilled water. Do not overfill. Replace the caps and reattach the negative battery cable. *Warning: Wash your hands thoroughly to remove any battery acid.*

Summary

Fluids in the automobile have critical functions. Fluids that are neglected and run low for long periods of time add stress to the various

💰 Price Guide

Oil
↳ $1.00 to $2.00 a quart
Antifreeze
↳ $4.00 to $8.00 a gallon
Automatic Transmission Fluid (ATF)
↳ $1.00 to $2.00 a quart
Manual Transmission Fluid/Differential Fluid (SAE 80W90)
↳ $2.00 to $4.00 a quart
Power Steering Fluid
↳ $1.50 to $3.00 a pint
Brake Fluid/Clutch Fluid
↳ $1.50 to $3.00 a 12 oz. bottle
Windshield Washer Fluid
↳ $1.00 to $2.00 a gallon
Distilled Water
↳ $0.50 to $1.00 a gallon
Windshield Wipers
↳ $5.00 to $10.00 a pair

components and can cause premature damage. Practice preventative maintenance by checking fluid levels frequently. Always refer to your owner's manual to identify the correct type of fluid for your specific vehicle. Using incorrect fluids can harm vital systems and could cause a hazardous situation while driving. Most of the fluids used in automobiles are toxic. Antifreeze has a sweet taste to animals and can be fatal if ingested. Dispose of all fluids properly. Always wash your hands thoroughly after checking and adding fluids.

💿 CD Activities

Fluid Level Check
• Fluid Level Check Activity
• Chapter 6 Study Questions

CHAPTER 7

Electrical System

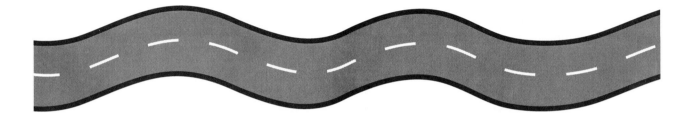

Contents

Introduction

The automotive electrical system consists of various wires, lights, circuits, fuses, relays, and switches. Even though the electrical system is extremely complex, there are still many repairs that you can do without taking your vehicle to a service facility. A simple thing like a headlight burning out can stop you from driving safely down the road. At some point in time most people will have to jump-start a vehicle, yet many are scared of the procedure. This chapter provides the basics of how to maintain, test, and repair various electrical system components.

Objectives

Upon completion of this chapter and activities on the CD, you should be able to:
- Define electricity in terms of voltage, current, and resistance.
- Identify and describe the components in the starting and charging system.
- Explain battery performance ratings.
- Identify the importance of fuses in the electrical system.
- Test the starter and alternator.
- Clean and test an automotive battery safely.
- Jump-start a vehicle safely.
- Change sealed beam and composite style headlamps.

Electrical Terms

Electricity can be defined as the movement of electrons in a conductor. Copper is a well known conductor. Electrons orbit the nucleus of an atom (*Figure 7.1*) much like the moon goes around the earth. Electricity flows through a conductor, which is usually in the form of a wire covered by an insulator. An insulator, such as plastic, is something that restricts the flow of electrons. Before discussing the electrical system, you need to be able to identify and describe three main terms:

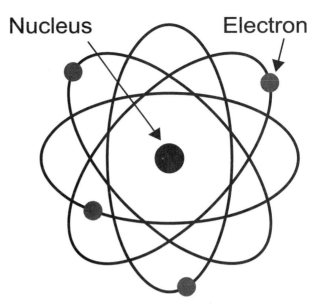

Nucleus   Electron

Figure 7.1   *Electron Orbit*

- Voltage
- Current
- Resistance

Voltage

A volt is the measure of voltage or pressure pushing electrons. Compare this to a faucet in your home. When the faucet is off there is still potential to flow, but the valve holds back the pressure. Voltage is the electrical pressure that causes current to flow. In technical terms, one volt is the amount of pressure required to move one ampere of current through a resistance of one ohm. (Amps and ohms will be discussed later.) Most vehicles have 12-volt systems, while most homes have 120-volt systems. Another difference in most home and vehicle electrical systems is the current. Automotive batteries are DC (Direct Current) while homes use AC (Alternating Current).

Current

Amperage is the unit used to measure electrical current. Current can be described as the quantity of electrons moving through a conductor. There are two types of electrical current: Direct Current (DC) and Alternating Current (AC). In DC systems the electrons are moving through the conductor in one direction. In AC systems the

Calculations

Ohm's Law Formula (V = I x R)

Current
x Resistance
= Voltage

electrons change direction at a given rate of time. The alternator in a vehicle generates AC, but then converts the current to DC to recharge the battery.

Resistance

An ohm is a measure of electrical resistance. The resistance in a circuit is usually a load such as a light, radio, electrical motor, or sensor. For example, there needs to be resistance in the filament of a light bulb for it to produce light. Ohm's Law shows the direct relationship between volts, amps, and ohms. Ohm's law states that: Voltage = Current x Resistance. This simple mathematical equation can be used to find one unknown variable if any two of the other variables are known.

Starting System

The starting system (*Figure 7.2*) converts chemical energy (molecular energy) to electrical energy (electrons moving through a conductor) to mechanical energy (energy of motion). The starting system consists of basically five components:

- Battery
- Key Switch
- Solenoid
- Starter
- Neutral Safety Switch

Battery

The purpose of the battery in a vehicle is to store chemical energy, supply electrical energy to the starter when the engine is cranking, and supplement the alternator in running various accessories (e.g., lights, radio, etc.). Most automotive batteries are 12 volts DC. The battery stores energy in a chemical form. In the starting system, the battery converts the chemical energy to electrical energy when the operator turns the key switch to start the engine.

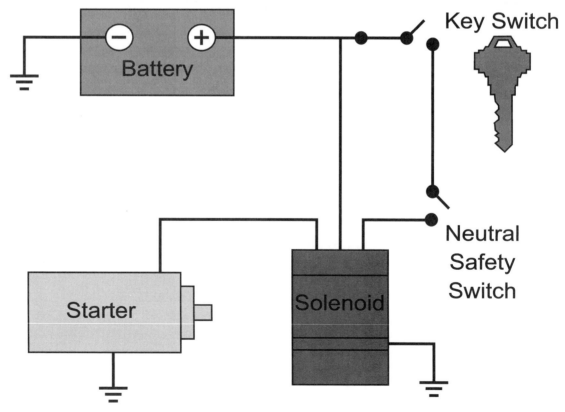

Figure 7.2   *Starting System Components*

Key Switch

A switch is a unit that can connect or disconnect electrical current from flowing. The key switch is the unit that is turned to start the engine. Usually located on the steering column, the key switch completes the circuit of electrical current to the starter solenoid.

Solenoid

A solenoid (*Figure 7.3*) is another type of switch. It is called an electromechanical switch. The key switch sends electrical current to the solenoid. Without the solenoid large amounts of current would have to go through the key switch. The solenoid is placed in the electrical circuit to switch from a low current to a high current. A small amount of electrical current energizes a coil within the solenoid, which creates a magnetic field. This closes the circuit for the higher current to go to the starter. The solenoid can either be located on the inside fender wall of the vehicle or mounted on or near the starter.

Figure 7.3   *Solenoid*

Starter

After the current goes through the solenoid it reaches the starter. The starter (*Figure 7.4*) is an energy converter. The starter converts electrical energy to mechanical energy to crank over the engine. The starter uses a small gear that meshes with the vehicle's flywheel gears. The flywheel is connected to the crankshaft. The starter is usually mounted on the underside of the engine.

🚑 Trouble Guide

Common Starting System Problems

- Worn out starter or solenoid
- Discharged battery
- Short circuited or broken wire

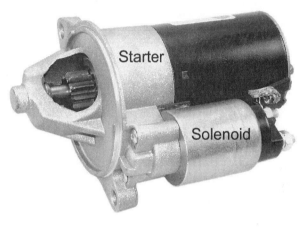

Figure 7.4   *Starter with Solenoid*

Neutral Safety Switch

The neutral safety switch only allows current to flow in the starting system if the clutch is depressed (manual transmission) or if the vehicle is in park or neutral (automatic transmission). This prevents the possibility of the vehicle being started while in gear.

✓ Tech Tip

Safe Starts

Get into the habit of always applying the parking brake when shutting off and parking a vehicle. Then when restarting the vehicle, leave the parking brake on while also firmly pressing on the brake pedal. This will minimize the risk of the vehicle moving upon start-up. On manual transmission vehicles, in addition to the above, be sure to engage the clutch.

Trouble Guide

Common Charging System Problems

- Belt is torn, glazed, cracked, loose
- Worn out alternator or regulator
- Short circuited or broken wire

Charging System

The charging system (*Figure 7.5*) is somewhat a reverse of the starting system. The charging system converts mechanical energy to electrical energy to chemical energy. The charging system keeps the battery recharged. The four main components of the charging system are:

- Alternator Drive Belt
- Battery
- Alternator
- Voltage Regulator

Alternator Drive Belt

The alternator drive belt turns the pulley on the alternator. Sometimes also referred to as a fan belt, the alternator drive belt may or may not be connected to other accessories such as the power steering pump, water pump, fan, air conditioning, and air pump. Belts come in two types: serpentine and "v". A serpentine belt (*Figure 7.6*), also called a multi-ribbed belt, is flat on one side and has grooves that run parallel with the belt.

✓ Tech Tip

Buying New Belts

When buying a new belt check the following: the number of accessories the belt goes around, if it is "v" or serpentine, and if the old belt has factory numbers on it to cross-reference.

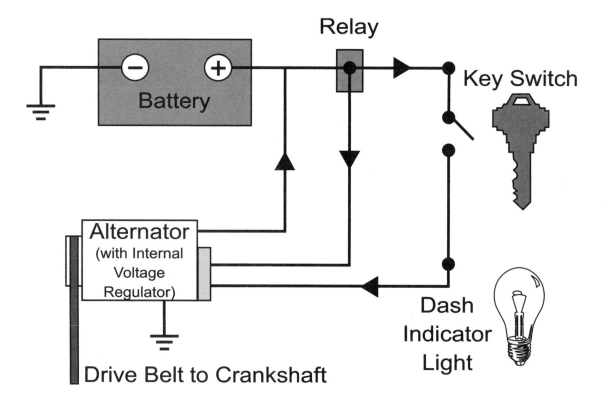

Figure 7.5

Charging System Components

Figure 7.6   **Serpentine Belt**

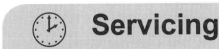

Servicing

Serpentine Belts
- Replace every 50,000 miles

Commonly, serpentine belts will have between 2 to 8 grooves on one side. Serpentine belts are usually ½ to 1 inch wide depending on the number of grooves and automotive application. In contrast, a v-belt (*Figure 7.7*) is usually less than ½ inch in width and has a cross-section that looks like a "v".

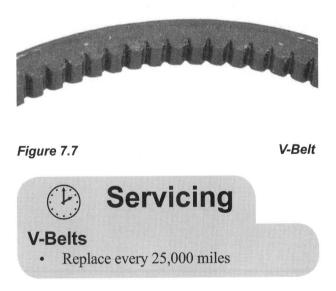

Figure 7.7   **V-Belt**

Servicing

V-Belts
- Replace every 25,000 miles

Battery

The battery is part of the charging system as well as the starting system. It is called a 12-volt DC battery, but actually should maintain about 12.6 volts when fully charged. The battery converts electrical energy to chemical energy (and vice versa). The battery stores energy for future use.

Alternator

The drive belt rotates the alternator pulley, which then turns a shaft in the alternator. The alternator (*Figure 7.8*) converts mechanical energy to electrical energy. Initially it converts the electricity to alternating current, but the end result is direct current. Diodes are used in the alternator to make the conversion from AC to DC current.

Figure 7.8   **Alternator**

✓ Tech Tip

Buying a New Alternator
When buying a new alternator, check the following: number of accessories (e.g., power windows, rear window defrosters, power seats), the wiring hookup, type of pulley, and the amperage rating stamped on the housing.

Voltage Regulator

The voltage regulator is commonly located in or near the alternator. It does basically what the name suggests; it regulates the electrical pressure (voltage). Common voltage from the regulator while the engine is running is 14.5 volts. If the regulator does not hold electrical pressure at or near 14.5 volts, the battery could be overcharged or undercharged by the alternator.

Battery Performance Ratings

When purchasing an automotive battery (*Figure 7.9*) it is important to identify the correct battery for your vehicle. Besides being the correct physical size, a battery must meet the amperage requirements to start the engine and run accessories. When comparing batteries from different vendors make sure you are comparing the same type of rating. Battery manufacturers basically use two ratings:

- Cold-Cranking Amps
- Cranking Amps

Figure 7.9   *Battery*

Cold-Cranking Amps

A battery that is rated with cold-cranking amps has been tested to deliver the specified number of amperes at 0 degrees Fahrenheit for a duration of 30 seconds.

⏲ Servicing

Battery
- Clean terminals twice a year

✓ Tech Tip

Batteries

You can clean batteries with a mixture of baking soda and water. See the lab procedure on the attached CD for details. When buying a new battery make sure you buy one with sufficient amperage rating (CCA or CA) and one that mounts safely in your vehicle. Many new batteries have top and side mount systems. Check to see how your old battery mounts in your vehicle.

Cranking Amps

A battery that is rated with cranking amps has been tested to deliver the specified number of amperes at 32 degrees Fahrenheit for a duration of 30 seconds.

🖱 Web Links

Automotive Parts Sites

AC Delco Replacement Parts
   ↳ www.acdelco.com
Advance Auto Parts and Service
   ↳ www.advanceautoparts.com
Auto Value Parts and Service
   ↳ www.autovalue.com
AutoZone Auto Parts
   ↳ www.autozone.com
CarQuest Auto Parts
   ↳ www.carquest.com
CSK Auto Inc. Parts and Service
   ↳ www.cskauto.com
J.C. Whitney Inc. Automotive Parts
   ↳ www.jcwhitney.com
NAPA Online Automotive Parts and Service
   ↳ www.napaonline.com
O'Reilly Automotive Inc. Parts and Service
   ↳ www.oreillyauto.com
Pep Boys Automotive Parts and Service
   ↳ www.pepboys.com

✓ Tech Tip

Fuses

Never replace a blown fuse with a higher amperage rated fuse, jumper wire, or steel stock to bypass the fuse completely. Severe electrical damage could result. The fuse needs to be the weak link in the circuit in order to protect all of the components.

Fuses

A junction block (*Figure 7.10*) containing fuses can be found under the dash or under the hood. A cover on the junction block often identifies the purpose of each fuse. If the cover is unclear, refer to your owner's manual for a fuse diagram. Fuses are used in electrical circuits to safeguard the vital components. A fuse will blow if too

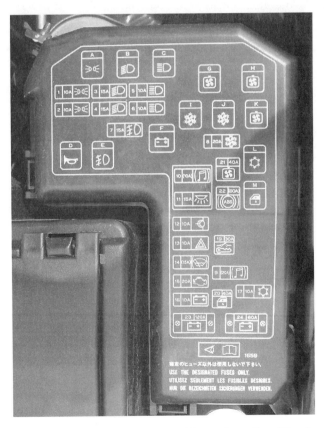

Figure 7.10   *Fuse Junction Block*

🚑 Trouble Guide

Fuse Continues to Blow

- Short circuited wire
- Accessory pulling too much current
- Wrong fuse rating

much current is trying to get to the intended load. Fuses are rated in amps such as: 5, 10, 15, 20, 25, 30, etc. Never replace a blown fuse with a larger amperage rating. A fuse is rated so it is the weakest link in the electrical circuit. If a blown fuse is replaced with a larger amp rated fuse severe electrical damage could result. Fuses can be broken down into two types: glass cylinder and blade style (*Figure 7.11*). Most vehicles from the

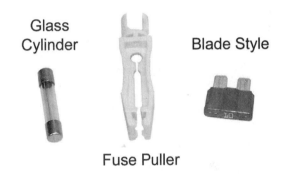

Figure 7.11   *Automotive Fuses*

1980s and newer use the blade style fuse. Some vehicles use a smaller blade style fuse called a mini-fuse. Always consult your owner's manual for fuse specifications.

🚑 Trouble Guide

Light Not Working

- Blown fuse
- Burned out bulb
- Loose wire

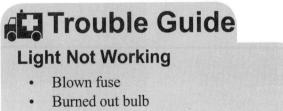

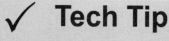

✓ Tech Tip

Bulbs

When replacing bulbs, use the number on the bulb as a guide. This is not true for most automotive replacement parts, but it is true for headlights and other bulbs.

Push in   Bayonet

Figure 7.12   ***Automotive Miniature Bulbs***

Lights

Lights are an important safety feature in a vehicle. Without them we could not see at night or notice when someone is braking or turning ahead. The activity on the attached CD will guide you in replacing and testing bulbs and headlamps. Lights burn out with age. Miniature light bulbs (e.g., taillights, brakelights, sidemarkers, etc.) come in various types: bayonet, screw-in, and push-in (***Figure 7.12***). Headlights usually come in two types: composite and sealed beam (***Figure 7.13***). When a light has the word *halogen* printed on it, it indicates that inside the bulb is a gas, which results in a brighter light.

✓ Tech Tip

Headlights

It is recommended to replace blown out headlights in pairs. Make sure if you are replacing a composite style headlight bulb that you do not touch the glass part. Oil from your fingers may shorten the life of the bulb. When replacing a sealed beam headlamp, do not remove the adjusting screws.

Sealed Beam Headlight Bulb

Composite
Headlight Bulb

Figure 7.13   ***Automotive Headlights***

💰 Price Guide

Miniature Light Bulb
↳ $1.00 to $2.00 each

Headlight - Sealed Beam or Composite
↳ $3.00 to $8.00 each

Fuse
↳ $0.50 to $3.00 each

Alternator Drive Belt
↳ $4.00 to $10.00 for "v"
↳ $20.00 to $40.00 for serpentine

Alternator
↳ $30.00 to $130.00

Starter
↳ $30.00 to $130.00

Solenoid
↳ $10.00 to $40.00

Battery
↳ $40.00 to $80.00

💿 CD Activities

Electrical System

- Starting Activity
- Charging Activity
- Battery Activity
- Jump-Starting Activity
- Lighting Activity
- Chapter 7 Study Questions

Summary

The electrical system may seem quite complex to the do-it-yourselfer, but there are simple ways to maintain it and save money. The starting system converts chemical energy to electrical energy to mechanical energy in order to start the engine. The charging system converts mechanical energy to electrical energy to chemical energy to recharge the battery. Fuses are over-current protection devices. Lights are used in many places on the automobile and periodically need replacing. The activities on the attached CD will assist you in testing and replacing automotive electrical system components and safely jump-starting a vehicle.

CHAPTER 8

Lubrication System

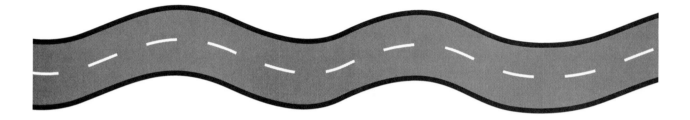

Contents

Introduction

The engine is the heart of your vehicle. Hundreds of moving parts within the engine must be lubricated. While the engine burns gasoline, it also takes in air from the outside. Thousands of gallons of air are brought into the engine for every gallon of gasoline consumed. Road dust and dirt are brought in with this air. While most of the air is cleaned, some dirt and dust may get by the air filter. In addition, incomplete combustion adds carbon deposits to the oil. Water can also come in contact with the oil from humidity in the air and from gaskets leaking. All of these factors can lead to engine oil failure. Engine oil is the substance that keeps your engine going day after day. It is extremely important to keep the oil clean and at the correct level to prevent engine oil failure.

✓ Tech Tip

Oil Warning Light

The engine warning light comes on when your engine has little or no oil pressure. Without oil pressure, severe engine damage can result. If the light stays on for more than 5 seconds, turn the engine off and check your oil. If it is at the correct level and the light still stays on, do not run the engine. Have a qualified service technician look into the problem.

Objectives

Upon completion of this chapter and activities on the CD, you should be able to:
- Define the purpose of oil in the lubricating system.
- Explain engine oil service and viscosity ratings.
- Discuss the advantages and disadvantages of synthetic oils.
- Discuss the importance of oil filters.
- Change the oil and filter on a vehicle.

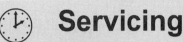

Servicing

Oil and Filter
- Change every 3 months or 3,000 miles

Purpose of Oil in the Lubricating System

Without oil an engine would not run. Engine oil is processed from crude oil and is specially formulated to do four main tasks within the engine:
- Lubricate
- Cool
- Clean
- Seal

Engine Oil Lubricates

The most important function that engine oil does is to lubricate. Within the engine there are hundreds of little parts rubbing up against each other. This rubbing creates friction. Friction is the force that resists motion between two bodies in contact. Engine oil molecules are like little ball bearings (*Figure 8.1*). The oil molecules have a tendency to stick to metal surfaces, but have less of a tendency to stick to each other. Oil decreases resistance and friction between two sliding bodies, resulting in a reduction of engine wear.

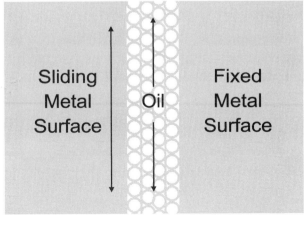

Figure 8.1   *Oil Lubrication*

Web Links

Oil Related Sites

AC Delco
↳ www.acdelco.com
American Petroleum Institute
↳ www.api.org
AMSOIL Synthetic Lubricants
↳ www.amsoil.com
BP Lubricants
↳ www.bp.com
Champion Laboratories Inc.
↳ www.champlabs.com
Chevron Lubricants
↳ www.chevron.com
Citgo Lubricants
↳ www.citgo.com
Exxon Lubricants
↳ www.exxon.com
Fram Filters
↳ www.fram.com
Motorcraft
↳ www.motorcraft.com
Society of Automotive Engineers
↳ www.sae.org
Wix Filters (Division of Dana)
↳ www.wixfilters.com

Engine Oil Cools

While engine oil does reduce friction, it obviously cannot eliminate it. Without engine oil, friction would build up undesirable heat, causing the engine to overheat, damaging internal components. Engine oil is pumped throughout the engine, moving into various parts and then back to the oil pan. In the oil pan or through an engine oil cooler, heat is dissipated to the outside air. Engine oil helps cool your engine in this process.

Engine Oil Cleans

The internal combustion engine is not very efficient (only about 28 cents of every dollar spent on fuel results in moving the vehicle). This inefficiency causes unburned deposits to build up within the engine. Some dirty air may also come in through the air filter during the intake process. While the engine oil is lubricating all the critical engine components, it also cleans by removing particles of carbon and dirt. As the oil is pumped throughout the engine, the dirty particles are screened out by the oil filter. Clean engine components help insure proper lubrication.

Engine Oil Seals

During engine operation, the pistons are rapidly moving up and down. Engine oil is also moving up and down with the pistons. Not only does engine oil lubricate, cool, and clean; it also seals between vital components. Engine oil seals between pistons and the cylinder walls to reduce blow-by. Blow-by is the gas that escapes past the piston rings and into the crankcase. Engine oil acts as a seal between components that are separated by gaskets. For example, you should put a thin film of oil on the oil filter gasket before installation to seal the connection between the filter and engine.

✓ Tech Tip

Overfilling Oil

If one is good then two is better, right? Not always. Engine oil contains detergents to help clean particles and other materials in the engine, similar to soap in a washing machine. If you overfill your engine oil, you will get air bubbles. Air does not have much of a lubricating ability. And adding too much oil can increase oil pressure causing failure to various seals and gaskets.

Understanding Oil Ratings

Reading an oil bottle can be very confusing. The three main ratings you need to become familiar with are (*Figure 8.2*):

- SAE – Society of Automotive Engineers
- API – American Petroleum Institute
- Energy Conserving

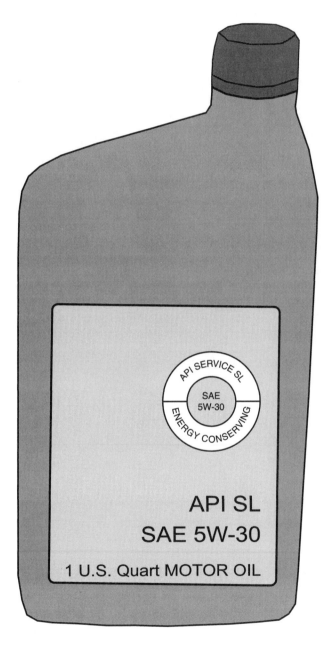

API SERVICE SL
SAE 5W-30
ENERGY CONSERVING

API SL
SAE 5W-30
1 U.S. Quart MOTOR OIL

Figure 8.2   *Quart of Oil with API, SAE, and Energy Conserving Ratings*

Society of Automotive Engineers

SAE rates engine oil viscosity. Viscosity is defined as the resistance to flow. Common viscosity ratings are SAE 10, SAE 30, SAE 5W30, SAE 10W30, SAE 10W40, and SAE 20W50. An oil that has two numbers in the rating is called a multi-grade oil. Multi-grade oils have been tested at various temperatures, and thus, can be used in a wide range of climates. The higher the viscosity number the thicker the oil. 5W30 oil acts like SAE 5 when cold and SAE 30 when warm. It is thin enough when the engine is cold and thick enough when the engine warms up. Light oil is used in cold climates and heavier oil is usually used in warmer climates. When the engine is cold the oil must be thin enough to get to all of the components, but when the engine warms up the oil must not be too thin as to enhance engine wear. This is why multi-grade oils have become so popular – they can fluctuate their viscosity with temperature changes. The most common engine oil viscosity rating for newer vehicles is 5W30, but always check the owner's manual for the manufacturer's recommendations.

 Trouble Guide

Excessive Oil Consumption

- Broken or worn piston rings
- Worn valve guides or seals
- Improper oil viscosity

American Petroleum Institute

API rates the engine oil service. SA, SB, SC, SD, SE, SF, SG, SH, SJ, and SL are API rated engine oils. The first letter "S" stands for spark ignition (gasoline) engines. Sometimes you'll see designations such as CH-4. The C stands for compression ignition (diesel) engines. The later the second letter is in the alphabet, the newer and more advanced the oil. For example, SC oil was used in vehicles in the 1960s. Newer engines are requiring more strenuous standards. When the American Petroleum Institute determines that current oils cannot meet newer engine needs or when current technology can improve engine oil qualities, it establishes a new set of standards. The key is that SL oils replace all the previous oils and can be used in any spark ignition engines with any of the previous letter designations. Look for the API symbol (*Figure 8.3*) when identifying the correct engine oil for your vehicle. In years to come, API will come out with more advanced oil standards to replace SL oils.

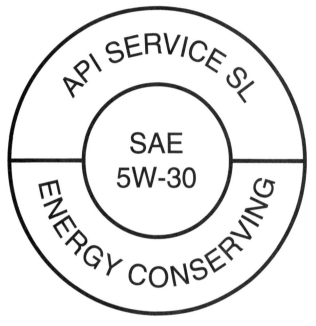

Figure 8.3   *API Symbol*

Energy Conserving

Energy conserving oils have increased additives to lower friction between components. By lowering the friction, the engine becomes more efficient which in turn improves fuel economy.

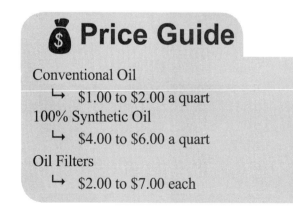

💰 Price Guide

Conventional Oil
 ↳ $1.00 to $2.00 a quart
100% Synthetic Oil
 ↳ $4.00 to $6.00 a quart
Oil Filters
 ↳ $2.00 to $7.00 each

🚑 Trouble Guide

Engine Oil Leaks

- Engine oil plug loose or not sealing
- Oil filter loose or not sealing
- Other various seals or gaskets leaking

Synthetic Oil

Synthetic oils are formulated from various chemicals and hydrocarbons to improve engine service and viscosity ratings. Even though synthetic oils have been used by the military since the 1950s, they became more common in the automotive sector in the 1990s. Synthetic oils have many pros and cons.

Advantages of Synthetic Oil

- Improves fuel mileage through increased lubricating qualities.
- Increases stability with less viscosity changes as temperatures fluctuate.
- Maintains lubricating qualities for up to 25,000 miles.

Disadvantages of Synthetic Oil

- Higher cost per quart of oil.
- Has a poor break in quality due to its high lubricating qualities. Usually not recommended for brand new engines.
- Most manufacturers still require regular oil change intervals.

With the various advantages and disadvantages the decision of using synthetic oil needs to be made by you and your vehicle manufacturer. It is important to check the manufacturer's warranty when considering synthetic oils.

Oil Filters

As oil circulates through the engine, it is filtered by an oil filter. The oil filter should be replaced every time your engine oil is changed. Oil filters (*Figure 8.4*) are composed of paper screening materials that collect dirt, dust, and other contaminants from the engine. Once the contaminants are removed from the engine oil, the oil is recirculated through the engine.

Figure 8.4   *Oil Filter*

Summary

Engine oil lubricates, cools, cleans, and seals engine components. While engine oil is a vital component to the longevity of an engine and may seem extremely complex, it is not very difficult to service. When purchasing oil look for the SAE and API ratings that meet the manufacturer's recommended requirements. Oil filters are used to remove contaminants from the engine oil. The activity on the attached CD will guide you in changing your oil and filter and disposing of them properly.

CD Activities

Lubrication System
- Oil and Filter Change Activity
- Chapter 8 Study Questions

CHAPTER 9

Fuel System

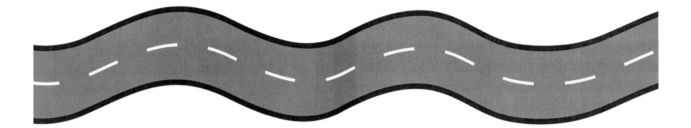

Contents

Figure 9.1   *Gas Station*

Introduction

Probably at least a couple of times a month you have to deal with filling up your vehicle's gas tank at a gas station (*Figure 9.1*). Most automobiles in production today depend on either gasoline or diesel. Many problems arise from using gasoline and diesel. Once they are burned, they are gone forever. That is the reality of today's fossil fuel driven society. Many simple things can be done to improve fuel mileage and efficiency of today's vehicles. This chapter discusses fuel properties, automotive fuel components, and ways to increase fuel efficiency.

Objectives

Upon completion of this chapter and activities on the CD, you should be able to:
- State gasoline and diesel properties.
- Explain the purpose of the fuel system.
- Describe the various parts of the fuel system.
- Identify ways to improve fuel economy.
- Discuss future alternatives to gasoline and diesel engines.

Gasoline Properties

Gasoline and diesel, like various other products (e.g., cosmetics, paints, soaps, nylon, and asphalt), come from crude oil. Crude oil is a nonrenewable energy resource. Crude oil, a fossil fuel, is an energy resource that will not be replenished over time. Examples of nonrenewable energy resources are coal, oil, and natural gas. Under current production and consumption rates, experts project oil to last 50-100 years. Crude oil goes through a distillation process at a refinery to form gasoline. Gasoline is a mixture of hydrocarbons (hydrogen and carbon) and is primarily used for internal combustion engines. Gasoline is the fuel that propels most of today's automobiles. Gasoline engines are considered spark ignition engines. The fuel needs to be ignited to burn in the engine. Gasoline properties that will be discussed are:
- Octane
- Knocking
- Additives

✓ Tech Tip

A Look to the Future

Due to the limited supplies of fossil fuels, oil companies and automobile manufacturers are looking for alternative fuels to propel vehicles. One type of fuel that is currently being used in specially designed vehicles is E-85. E-85 fuel is 85% ethanol (grain) based. Another promising fuel is hydrogen. Hydrogen fuel cells are devices that convert hydrogen and oxygen to water. During this process electricity is produced to propel the vehicle. With only water as a by-product, hydrogen fuel cell vehicles produce no harmful emissions.

Figure 9.2 *Common Octane Ratings*

Octane

When pulling up to a gas pump, you usually have a couple of choices. Pumps are commonly labeled *regular*, *mid-grade*, or *premium*. What does this mean? For the most part, it relates to the octane rating in the gasoline. Octane is defined as a resistance to burning. The higher the octane number, the more the fuel resists burning. The more the fuel resists burning, the more complete the combustion is when the fuel ignites. Usually higher compression engines need higher octane fuels. Common octane numbers are regular 87, mid-grade (or plus) 89, and premium 93 (*Figure 9.2*). The octane requirement depends on the engine design, the altitude the vehicle is driven at, and the way the individual drives. Most automobiles require a minimum of 87 octane, but always check the owner's manual.

Knocking

Many people have experienced an engine knocking or pinging during acceleration. This sound is created when fuel ignites prematurely. Anti-knock characteristics relate directly to octane ratings. The higher the octane rating the more the fuel resists knocking. It takes a higher temperature and more compression to ignite a fuel with a higher octane.

Additives

In many parts of the country deicers, such as isopropyl alcohol, are added to gasoline to prevent gas lines from freezing. Rust inhibitors are added to help volatile metals resist rusting. Detergents are added to clean the fuel system. Many cities have mandated the use of ethanol as an additive. Often up to 10% of gasoline is ethanol. Ethanol is a grain alcohol, commonly made from corn or other starch rich grains. When gasoline and ethanol are mixed, it is called gasohol. Gasohol burns cleaner, emitting less air pollutants and greenhouse gases, than 100% gasoline.

Diesel Properties

Some people think diesel fuel is only used in semi-tractors (*Figure 9.3*) or heavy equipment. However, there are many diesel cars and light trucks on the highway today. Diesel fuel is also a product of distilling (separating and vaporizing)

Figure 9.3 *Semi-tractor Car Hauler*

crude oil. At different temperatures of the distillation process, different products are collected. Diesel fuel actually has more energy per volume than gasoline. Diesel engines are called compression ignition engines. They do not need spark plugs to ignite fuel. The high compression (about 20:1 compared to about 9:1 in gasoline engines) and heat in the combustion chamber ignites the fuel. Diesel engines have glow plugs that heat the combustion chamber just prior to starting. Diesel properties that will be discussed are:

- Cetane Number
- Grades of Diesel

Cetane Number

The cetane number is much like the octane number in gasoline. The cetane number relates to how well fuel ignites. The higher the cetane number, the better the ignition quality of fuel. Cetane numbers of 40 to 50 are the most common.

Grades of Diesel

Two types of diesel fuels are used in cars and trucks: Number 1 and Number 2. The American Society for Testing Materials (ASTM) classifies these two grades. In the distillation process, No. 1 diesel fuel has a lower boiling point than No. 2 and thus vaporizes easier than No. 2. Therefore, No. 1 diesel fuel is commonly used when the outside ambient temperature is abnormally low. In the northern climates of the United States many gas stations commonly provide No. 1 in the winter, a mixture of No. 1 and No. 2 in the fall and spring, and No. 2 in the summer. No. 2 diesel fuel has a tendency to "gel" in severely cold climates.

Purpose of the Fuel System

Fuel is added to the gas tank from a gas station. The fuel (chemical energy) is stored in the gas tank for future use. The fuel is then pumped to the carburetor or injection system. The carburetor or the injection system mixes the fuel with air. The best air to fuel mixture is about 14.7 parts of air to 1 part of fuel. The mixture is brought into

the combustion chamber and burned. The purpose of the fuel system is to store, transfer, and then to mix the fuel with air.

⛑ Trouble Guide

Engine Lacks Power (sluggish)
- Clogged fuel filter
- Impurities in fuel
- Fuel octane too low

Parts of the Fuel System

The fuel system parts that will be discussed are:
- Fuel (Gas) Cap
- Fuel Tank
- Fuel Pump
- Fuel Lines
- Carburetor or Injection System
- Air Filter
- PCV Valve
- Fuel Filter
- CCV Filter

Fuel Cap

The fuel (gas) cap (*Figure 9.4*) keeps the fuel from spilling out, releases the vacuum that is created as fuel is drawn into the engine, releases pressure as the gasoline expands and contracts with changing temperatures, and keeps foreign objects from entering the fuel tank.

Figure 9.4   *Fuel Cap*

Fuel Tank

The fuel (gas) tank, made of either steel or plastic (*Figure 9.5*), stores the fuel for later use.

Figure 9.5   *Fuel Tank*

Fuel Pump

The fuel pump, either mechanical (*Figure 9.6*) or electrical, supplies the engine with fuel. Mechanical fuel pumps are usually located on the engine and are commonly used with carburetor type vehicles. Electrical fuel pumps are usually located in the fuel tank and are commonly used with fuel injected vehicles.

Figure 9.6   *Mechanical Fuel Pump*

Fuel Lines

Fuel lines, made of either steel or rubber, carry the fuel to the carburetor or fuel injectors.

Carburetor or Injection System

Cars have either a carburetor or fuel injection system to mix the fuel with air. Most vehicles today have fuel injectors. Fuel injectors can be two types: throttle body or port. In a throttle body injection system, usually one fuel injector is used to supply fuel to all of the engine's cylinders. In a port injection system, there is one fuel injector for each cylinder.

Air Filter

Air filters (*Figure 9.7*) clean dirt and dust from the air that is being drawn into the engine. Thousands of gallons of air are drawn into the engine per gallon of gasoline burned. A dirty air filter can cause low fuel efficiency by "choking out" (decreasing the air-fuel ratio) the engine. Dirty air can also cause premature failure to vital engine components (e.g., bearings, valves, and piston rings).

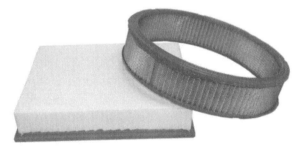

Figure 9.7   *Air Filters*

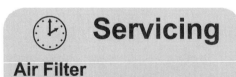

Servicing

Air Filter
- Change every 12,000 miles or as recommended by the manufacturer

PCV Valve

The positive crankcase ventilation (PCV) valve (*Figure 9.8*) reduces air pollution, increases fuel economy, and recirculates excess gas. The PCV valve reduces the air pressure within the engine. A plugged valve reduces fuel efficiency and increases your vehicle's emissions.

Figure 9.8   *PCV Valve*

⏱ Servicing

PCV Valve
- Change every 2 years, 24,000 miles, or as recommended by the manufacturer

Fuel Filter

The fuel filter (*Figure 9.9*), located between the fuel tank and the carburetor or injection system, cleans the fuel entering the engine. The fuel filter may be located under the vehicle near a frame member or under the hood near the carburetor or fuel injectors. Fuel filters have a paper type element in them to collect dirt. Clogged fuel

✓ Tech Tip

Changing the Fuel Filter

When changing the fuel filter on your vehicle, it is important to avoid getting fuel on your skin or in your eyes. All fuel system services should be done in a well-ventilated area with the engine cool. It is also important to relieve fuel pressure. Some vehicles with fuel injection systems run as high as 85 PSI (pounds per square inch) of fuel pressure. Always where safety goggles.

filters slow fuel delivery, lower the performance of the engine, and cause excessive wear on the fuel pump.

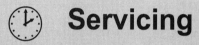

Figure 9.9   *Fuel Filter*

⏱ Servicing

Fuel Filter
- Change every 2 years, 24,000 miles, or as recommended by the manufacturer

CCV Filter

The crankcase ventilation filter (*Figure 9.10*) is usually placed inside the air filter housing and is connected to the PCV valve via a tube or hose. (CCV filter is sometimes called the PCV inlet filter.) This filter cleans the air going into the engine's crankcase.

Figure 9.10   *CCV Filter*

⏱ Servicing

CCV Filter
- Change every 2 years, 24,000 miles, or as recommended by the manufacturer

💰 Price Guide

Regular Unleaded Gasoline
↳ $1.50 to $2.20 a gallon
Air Filter
↳ $3.00 to $15.00 each
Fuel Filter
↳ $3.00 to $15.00 each
Fuel Pump
↳ $20.00 to $50.00 each
PCV Valve
↳ $3.00 to $8.00 each
CCV Filter
↳ $3.00 to $8.00 each

Improving Fuel Economy

Several things contribute to good fuel economy. Over time, new technology has contributed to better fuel and fuel delivery methods. The do-it-yourselfer can improve fuel economy by:

- Checking tire pressure
- Tuning-up the engine
- Checking the wheel alignment
- Running air conditioning only when necessary
- Changing the oil as required
- Checking cooling system operation
- Looking for dragging brakes
- Avoiding excessive idling
- Combining trips
- Moderating speed

Tire Pressure

Probably the most overlooked and the easiest thing to check regularly is tire pressure. Low tire pressure causes more frictional resistance on the highway. This reduces fuel economy and increases tire wear. Having incorrect tire pressure can also increase the chances of having a dangerous blowout.

Tune-ups

A properly tuned engine (replacing ignition components such as spark plugs and replacing fuel related components such as the air filter) can improve your fuel mileage. An improperly running engine can waste up to 15% of additional gasoline.

Wheel Alignment

If the wheels are not contacting the road surface properly, fuel mileage will decrease due to increased friction.

Air Conditioning

Running extra accessories puts more load on the engine, requiring more fuel.

Oil Changes

Changing the oil as required by the manufacturer increases fuel economy. Clean engine oil has better cooling, cleaning, lubricating, and sealing properties than dirty oil.

Cooling System

If the engine is running too cool, it can lower fuel economy. The proper thermostat and periodical flushing will assure proper operation.

Brakes

If the brakes are dragging or rubbing slightly, they can cause more frictional resistance for the engine to overcome, reducing fuel economy.

✓ Tech Tip

Excessive Idling

Often vehicles are left to idle. Short idling, such as sitting at a stoplight, is not a problem. But an engine left idling for an hour can burn three gallons of gas, adding unnecessary pollution to our atmosphere. A well-tuned vehicle does not require a lot of fuel to start. It is much more efficient to turn off your engine instead of letting it idle for long periods of time.

Avoid Excessive Idling

If your vehicle is not moving, you are getting zero miles to the gallon. It is much better for the environment and for your pocketbook to shut off your car if you plan to sit for an extended period of time.

✓ Tech Tip

Improving Fuel Economy

- Avoid jack rabbit starts
- Use cruise control
- Remove excess weight
- Fill up when it is cool outside
- Avoid resting foot on brake pedal
- Put the transmission in overdrive
- Plan trips

Combine Trips

One of the best ways to increase fuel economy and the life of your engine is to plan ahead. Short trips are hard on engines. On short trips engines do not have time to reach the most optimal operating temperature, causing poor fuel economy. Combining short errands will also put fewer miles on your vehicle.

Moderate Speed

Most vehicles receive the best fuel economy at 55 miles per hour (*Figure 9.11*). Also it is important to avoid abrupt accelerations and decelerations. "Stop and go" traffic reduces fuel economy dramatically. Using your cruise control to keep your speed constant on the highway will also increase your fuel economy.

🚑 Trouble Guide

Excessive Fuel Consumption

- Dirty air filter
- Low tire pressure

Figure 9.11   *Speed Limit Sign*

🖱 Web Links

Fuel Related Sites

United States Department of Energy
↳   www.energy.gov
Chevron Corporation
↳   www.chevron.com
Shell Oil Company
↳   www.countonshell.com
British Petroleum
↳   www.bp.com
Holley Performance Products Inc.
↳   www.holley.com
Exxon/Mobil
↳   www.exxonmobil.com
Conoco/Phillips
↳   www.conocophillips.com
National Ethanol Vehicle Coalition
↳   www.e85fuel.com
Fuel Cells
↳   www.fuelcells.org

Fuel Prices

Fuel prices first became a concern in the 1970s, but have gained attention once again. Even though technology is advancing fuel efficiency, much of the public has decided to buy gas-guzzling vehicles (e.g., sport utility vehicles). Every year more and more vehicles are put on the highways consuming more and more fuel. If the supply of fuel decreases and fuel demand increases, prices will surely rise. Contrary to belief, fuel is only marked up about 5% at retail outlets. The local service station/convenience store makes about 8-10 cents on every gallon of gas sold.

Summary

When pulling up to a gas pump, it is important to supply your engine with the fuel that the automotive manufacturer recommends. The purpose of the fuel system is to store, transfer, and then mix the fuel with air. In a gasoline engine, the lower the octane number the more likely the engine will knock. Gasoline engines are spark ignition engines. Diesel engines are compression ignition engines. Diesel fuel comes in two grades: No. 1 and No. 2. The outside temperature determines the type of diesel to use – No. 2 in warm weather and No. 1 in cold weather. Various parts of the fuel system work together to supply clean fuel and air to the engine. Fuel economy can increase through tune-ups, correct tire pressure, regular oil changes, and moderating your speed.

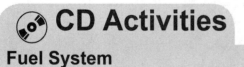 **CD Activities**

Fuel System
- Fuel System Activity
- Chapter 9 Study Questions

CHAPTER 10

Cooling System

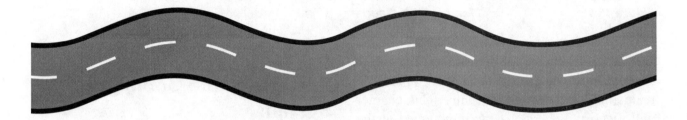

Contents

Introduction

Thousands of automobiles are stranded on the side of the road due to cooling system problems each year. Precautions can be taken to avoid this, including paying attention to the temperature gauge (*Figure 10.1*). Engine coolant, in addition

Figure 10.1   *Temperature Gauge*

to oil, carries away excess heat from the engine. Too much heat can destroy an engine, while an engine that is not at the proper operating temperature will run inefficiently. This chapter will identify and discuss the importance of the cooling system, maintenance procedures, and cooling system component identification.

✓ Tech Tip

Temperature Light

This engine warning light comes on when your engine has reached a potentially damaging temperature. Overheating an engine can warp and crack cylinder heads, overheat the engine oil, and cause excessive stress on engine components. If the temperature light stays on (or the gauge is in the HOT range), pull over to the side of the road and let the engine cool.

Objectives

Upon completion of this chapter and activities on the CD, you should be able to:
- Identify the purpose of the cooling system.
- List and describe the components in the cooling system.
- Define coolant properties.
- Explain how coolant flows through an engine.
- Test and service the cooling system.

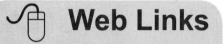

Web Links

Cooling System Related Sites
Hypertech Inc.
 ↳   www.hypertech-inc.com
Stant Corporation
 ↳   www.stant.com
Prestone
 ↳   www.prestone.com
Gates Rubber Company
 ↳   www.gates.com
Peak Antifreeze
 ↳   www.peakantifreeze.com

Purpose of the Cooling System

The cooling system is designed to do three things:
- Maintain efficient operating temperature.
- Remove excess engine heat.
- Reach operating temperature quickly.

Maintain Operating Temperature

On today's computer controlled vehicles it is vital to maintain an efficient operating temperature. Too low of a temperature will cause the computer to run the vehicle with a rich air-fuel mixture. Too high of a temperature and the engine will warp metal and crack gaskets, which could eventually lead to major engine damage. Most vehicles run coolant at a temperature of around 200 degrees Fahrenheit. Coolant temperature is controlled by a thermostat, which will be discussed later in this chapter.

Removes Excess Heat

Temperatures of the metal around the combustion chamber (where the fuel is ignited) can reach extremely high temperatures. Coolant flows throughout the engine to remove this excess heat and transfer it to the radiator where it is eventually cooled.

Water Pump

The water pump (*Figure 10.2*) is attached to the engine block. Its main purpose is to keep the coolant circulating. It draws cooled coolant in from the lower radiator hose and pushes it through the engine. An engine drive belt ("v" or serpentine) rotates most water pumps.

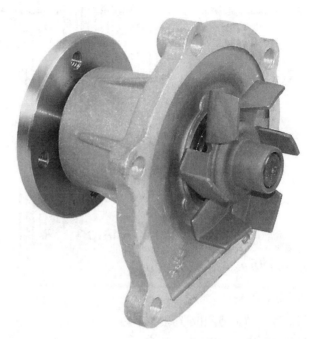

Figure 10.2   **Water Pump**

🚚 Trouble Guide

Engine Overheating

- Coolant low
- Improper coolant mixture
- Clogged radiator fins
- Faulty thermostat (stuck closed)
- Restricted radiator hose
- Fan not working
- Faulty temperature sensor
- Faulty water pump
- Drive belt loose
- Faulty radiator cap

Reach Operating Temperature

Gasoline is wasted every second the engine runs below the most efficient operating temperature. The electronic control module communicates with the temperature sensor and regulates the other systems based on the coolant temperature. An engine running at the proper temperature will run cleaner, smoother, and more efficient than an engine running too cool or too hot.

🚚 Trouble Guide

Engine Overcooling

- Faulty thermostat (stuck open)
- Faulty temperature sensor

Cooling System Components

The following cooling system components will be discussed:

- Water Pump
- Radiator
- Thermostat
- Radiator and Heater Hoses
- Radiator Cap
- Radiator Fan
- Drive Belts
- Coolant Recovery Tank

💰 Price Guide

Thermostat
↳ $2.00 to $8.00 each
Water Pump
↳ $30.00 to $50.00 each
Upper and Lower Radiator Hoses
↳ $7.00 to $15.00 each
Hose Clamps
↳ $0.50 to $1.00 each
Antifreeze
↳ $6.00 to $10.00 a gallon
Radiator Cap
↳ $7.00 to $15.00 each

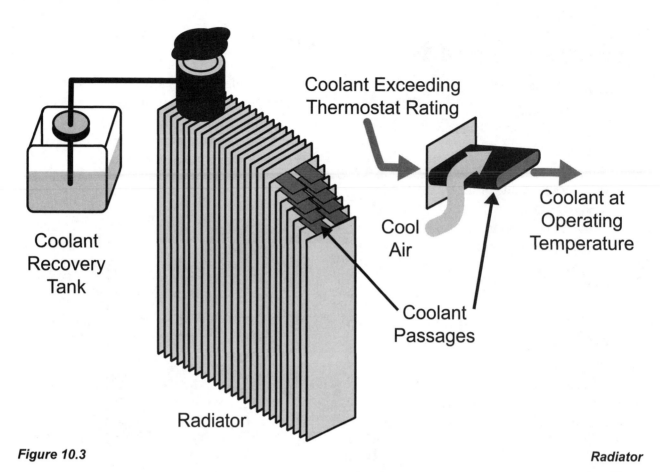

Figure 10.3   *Radiator*

Radiator

The purpose of the radiator (*Figure 10.3*) is to remove heat from the coolant. Hot coolant enters the radiator by the upper radiator hose when the temperature of the coolant reaches the opening rating of the thermostat. The coolant runs down through various tubes. Air is drawn around the radiator tubes by a fan and by the motion of the vehicle. The air flow cools the coolant in the radiator tubes so it can be returned to the engine.

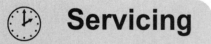

Servicing

Thermostat
• Change every 2 years or as recommended by the manufacturer

Thermostat

The thermostat (*Figure 10.4*) is the brain of the cooling system. It senses the temperature of the coolant and allows the fluid to exit to the radiator. The thermostat controls the temperature in the cooling system. Thermostats are rated at a specified temperature – usually between 180 to 195 degrees Fahrenheit. When an engine is cold, the thermostat is closed. Once the engine temperature reaches the thermostat rating, the thermostat opens.

Figure 10.4   *Thermostat*

Hoses

Two main hoses attach the radiator to the engine. These hoses (*Figure 10.5*) are called the upper and lower radiator hoses. Cooled coolant is transferred from the radiator to the engine through the lower hose. Hot coolant is returned to the radiator by the upper hose. The upper hose usually connects to the water outlet that covers the thermostat. The lower hose connects to the water pump. Heater hoses are used to transport heated coolant to the heater core (basically a mini-radiator). The heater core is located on the engine compartment's firewall. The heater fan, controlled by the operator, can blow air through the heater core providing heat inside the vehicle on cold days.

Figure 10.5   **Radiator Hose**

Servicing

Radiator Hoses
- Change every 4 years, 48,000 miles, or as recommended by the manufacturer

Radiator Cap

The radiator cap (*Figure 10.6*) is designed to maintain a constant pressure in the cooling system. Most pressure caps are rated between 8

Figure 10.6   **Radiator Cap**

to 16 PSI. PSI stands for pounds per square inch. Increasing pressure on the cooling system also increases the boiling point of the coolant. The radiator cap allows expanding coolant to go to the coolant recovery tank. When the fluid has cooled, it is drawn back into the radiator.

Radiator Fan

Radiator fans draw air through the radiator to cool the coolant. Fans are either mechanically or electrically driven. A mechanical fan is driven by a belt. An electrical fan is driven by an electric motor. Most newer vehicles use an electric fan because it is more efficient and more suitable for front-wheel drive vehicles with transverse engines.

Drive Belts

Drive belts turn water pumps, mechanical fans, power steering pumps, and air conditioning compressors. Automotive drive belts (*Figure 10.7*) are connected to the crankshaft pulley that

Figure 10.7   **Serpentine Drive Belt**

turns from the reciprocating motion of the engine. Worn or loose belts can cause slippage. Belt slippage can lead to an engine overheating.

Coolant Recovery Tank

The coolant recovery tank (also called the expansion bottle) (*Figure 10.8*) holds excess coolant during the cooling system operation. As pressure and heat build up, the coolant expands and is then transferred to the recovery tank. This allows no fluid loss during cooling system operation, while keeping the maximum amount of coolant in the system at all times. Another advantage of using a coolant recovery tank is to keep outside air from being drawn into the engine block. Air, carrying in outside contaminants, can cause rust in cooling system components.

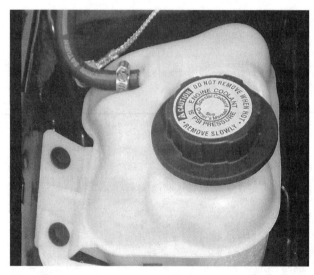

Figure 10.8　　　　**Coolant Recovery Tank**

Coolant Properties

Mainly two types of coolant are sold for automotive use: standard antifreeze and extended life antifreeze. Standard antifreeze, green in color, was most commonly used in vehicles prior to 1995. Extended life coolants, such as Dex-Cool, are usually orange in color. Dex-Cool is a type of antifreeze common in 1995 and newer GM vehicles. As presented in Chapter 6, *Fluid Level Check*, antifreeze can come in various colors. Always refer to your owner's manual to identify

⏲ Servicing

Standard Antifreeze (green)
* Change every 2 years or 24,000 miles
* Test once a year

the correct antifreeze to use in your vehicle. Both standard antifreeze (green) and extended life antifreeze are ethylene glycol based, which is toxic. The main differences between standard and extended life antifreeze are the rust inhibitors and additives used. Recently some manufacturers started producing more environmentally friendly antifreeze products that are propylene glycol based. These products are not as harmful to pets, wildlife, or humans if accidentally ingested. Coolant within an engine does three main things:
* Prevents freezing and boiling.
* Lubricates the water pump.
* Inhibits corrosion.

⏲ Servicing

Dex-Cool Antifreeze
* Change every 5 years or 150,000 miles
* Test once a year

Freezing and Boiling

Pure water should not be used to cool an engine. A couple of problems exist with using pure water. Water freezes at 32 degrees Fahrenheit and boils at 212 degrees Fahrenheit. Vehicles in some parts of the country are driven in temperatures below 32 degrees Fahrenheit. If coolant freezes, it will expand and eventually crack the engine block. Also, the engine can run hotter than 212 degrees Fahrenheit. If the coolant boils it causes problems. The solution to this is to use an antifreeze/water mixture. In most climates a 50% water to 50% antifreeze mixture is recommended. This will give the coolant a freezing point of –35 degrees Fahrenheit and a boiling point of

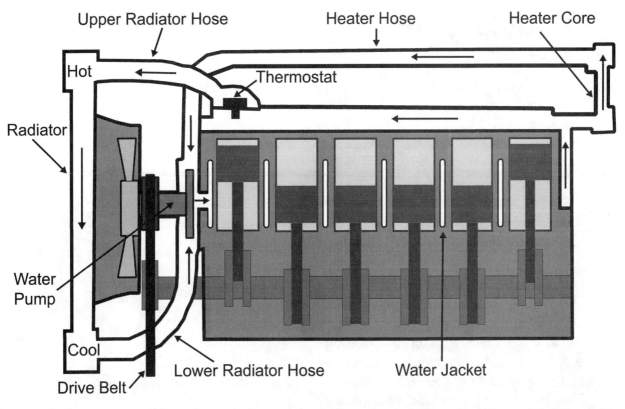

Figure 10.9   *Coolant Flow in an Inline 6 Engine*

about 225 degrees Fahrenheit. In a severely cold climate, 60% antifreeze to 40% water is necessary. It is not recommended to use pure antifreeze in the coolant system. The antifreeze/water mixture carries the best properties.

Lubricates

The coolant mixture lubricates bearings that are located inside the water pump. As antifreeze ages, its lubricating ability lessens.

> ## ✓ Tech Tip
>
> ### Used Coolant
>
> Used coolant is considered a hazardous waste. Bring the coolant to a service center that recycles it or wait until your community has a hazardous waste pickup day. If you have to store the coolant, do not leave it in open pans where pets or children can get into it.

Inhibits Corrosion

Bare engine components are susceptible to corrosion. Coolant contains chemicals to minimize rust and corrosion from taking place inside the engine.

Coolant Flow

The water pump causes coolant to flow (*Figure 10.9*) throughout the engine. Coolant travels in passageways called water jackets. Coolant is moved from the radiator, through the lower radiator hose, to the water pump, to the numerous water jackets, to the thermostat, through the upper radiator hose, and back to the radiator. Coolant is separated from the engine oil and combustion chamber by gaskets and seals.

🚑 Trouble Guide

Coolant Loss

- Defective seal or gasket
- Hole in radiator
- Hole in hose
- Engine overheating and boiling over
- Loose hose clamp

Summary

The cooling system is extremely important to the operation of the engine. Without it, the engine block could actually melt. The three purposes of the cooling system are to maintain efficient engine-operating temperature, remove excess heat, and to bring the engine up to operating temperature as quickly as possible. Antifreeze prevents the coolant from freezing, increases the boiling temperature, lubricates components within the engine, and reduces the likelihood of corrosion.

💿 CD Activities

Cooling System

- Cooling System Activity
- Chapter 10 Study Questions

CHAPTER 11

Ignition System

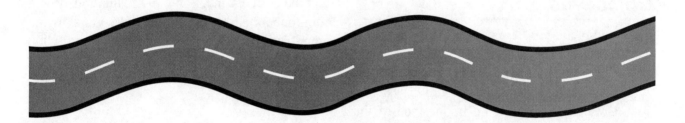

Contents

Introduction

The engine in a vehicle needs three things to run: fuel, air, and spark. Chapter 9, *Fuel System*, presented how the engine receives fuel and air, now it is time for the spark. The ignition system on vehicles has changed over the years, but its purpose has been the same – to ignite the fuel-air mixture. The ignition converts chemical energy of the fuel into wanted mechanical energy of motion and wasted thermal energy. This chapter gives you the knowledge to identify and perform basic maintenance procedures on a vehicle's ignition system.

Objectives

Upon completion of this chapter and activities on the CD, you should be able to:

- Define the purpose of the ignition system.
- Identify the generations of ignition systems.
- Define and discuss the importance of the ignition system components while relating them to their respective generation.
- Test and perform basic service procedures on the ignition system.

Purpose of the Ignition System

As mentioned earlier, fuel, air, and spark must all be present for the engine to run. The purpose of the ignition system is to:

- Step up voltage.
- Ignite the fuel-air mixture efficiently and in a timely matter.

Step Up Voltage

One of the purposes of the ignition system is to step up voltage. Basic electrical principles were presented in Chapter 7, *Electrical System*. You know now that automotive batteries have a surface voltage of about 12 volts DC. This is sufficient for running accessories such as lights and radios, but not powerful enough to ignite the air-fuel mixture within the combustion chamber. Common voltages at the spark plug can range from about 10,000 to 50,000 volts. These high voltages are created with a coil, a step up transformer.

Ignition

Automotive engines are considered four-stroke engines (intake, compression, power, and exhaust). To get to the stroke that is wanted, the power stroke (that's the one that gives the vehicle power to move), the engine must cycle through the other necessary strokes. In addition to this, most automotive engines have 4 to 8 pistons working together to provide the mechanical energy. Not only does the ignition system have to ignite the fuel-air mixture, it also needs to ignite it at the correct time. Some of the ignition system components carry low voltage (12 volts) while others support high voltages (10,000 to 50,000 volts). The ignition system is designed to monitor and control the ignition to make the vehicle run smoothly.

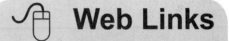 **Web Links**

Ignition System Related Sites
MSD Ignition (Autotronic Control Corp.)
↳ www.msdignition.com
Mr. Gasket Company (ACCEL Wires)
↳ www.mrgasket.com
AutoZone Automotive Parts
↳ www.autozone.com
Standard Motor Products Inc.
↳ www.smpcorp.com
SparkPlugs.Com
↳ www.sparkplugs.com
SplitFire Spark Plugs
↳ www.splitfire.com
NGK Spark Plugs
↳ www.ngksparkplugs.com
Autolite Spark Plugs
↳ www.autolite.com

Generations of the Ignition System

Over the years automotive manufacturers have come a long way in making the "power" (ignition) stroke more efficient. This has been done by advancements in technology. The purpose over the years has been the same: to increase the voltage that induces a spark. Modern technology has made the power stroke more reliable and efficient. It should be noted that the following dates of the ignition generations are approximated. Depending on the automotive manufacturer, the implementation time of the ignition system generation may vary. The generations of the ignition system are commonly divided into the following eras:

*   Conventional Ignition System
*   Electronic Ignition System
*   Distributorless Ignition System

Conventional Ignition System

The conventional ignition system was common in vehicles from about 1920 to the mid 1970s. This system is sometimes considered a mechanical type ignition system. Tune-ups during this age were frequent – sometimes every 5,000 to 10,000 miles. Common components in the conventional ignition include the battery, ignition coil, condenser (*Figure 11.1*), contact points (*Figure 11.1*), distributor cap, distributor rotor, spark plug wires, and spark plugs.

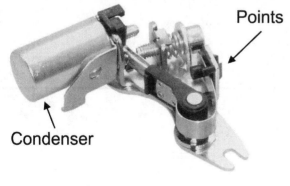

Figure 11.1   *Contact Points and Condenser*

Trouble Guide
Engine Will Not Start (but does rotate)
*   Moisture on ignition system components
*   Worn or incorrectly gapped spark plugs
*   Faulty ignition module or coil
*   Cracked, burned, or corroded distributor cap or rotor

Electronic Ignition System

The electronic ignition system was common in vehicles from about 1975 to the early 1990s. Tune-ups during this age were required about every 25,000 miles. Common components in the electronic ignition system include the battery, ignition coil, ignition module, distributor cap, distributor rotor, spark plug wires, and spark plugs. The main advantage over the conventional ignition is the elimination of the contact points that physically rub on the distributor shaft. This elimination decreased the number of components that needed servicing. The ignition module (*Figure 11.2*) in electronic ignition systems controls the spark.

Figure 11.2   *Ignition Module*

Distributorless Ignition System

The distributorless ignition system was actually introduced in the mid 1980s, but really became popular in the early 1990s. Some manufacturers call this a direct ignition system. Tune-up intervals on the distributorless ignition systems vary, but some manufacturer's boast up to 100,000 miles. Common components in the distributorless ignition system include the battery, individual ignition coils, electronic control module, spark plug wires, spark plugs, crankshaft sensor, and camshaft sensor. The advantages over the electronic ignition are the elimination of a mechanical distributor, increased voltage at the spark plug, better timed spark, and a more efficient running engine.

Ignition System Components

Changing technology has made major advancements in many parts of the ignition system. Over time some components were eliminated, others were added, while others stayed pretty much the same. The following is a list of the most common components on modern day vehicles:

- Battery
- Ignition Coil or Coil Packs
- Ignition Module
- Distributor Cap and Rotor
- Spark Plug Wires
- Spark Plugs
- Crankshaft and Camshaft Sensors

Battery

The battery (*Figure 11.3*), used in all three ignition generations, is a critical component in many systems: electrical, starting, charging, and the ignition. Electrical energy must be present to ignite the air-fuel mixture. The problem is that a 12-volt battery does not have enough push (electrical pressure) to create the spark that is

Figure 11.3   *Automotive Battery*

necessary in the combustion chamber, but it is the starting point of power.

Ignition Coil

The ignition coil (*Figure 11.4*), used on all three generations, steps up the low voltage to the high voltage needed to ignite the air-fuel mixture. The conventional and electronic generations usually had one coil, while the distributorless generation has coil packs – a series of coils to induce voltage for each individual cylinder.

Figure 11.4   *Ignition Coil*

💰 Price Guide

Spark Plugs
↳ $1.00 to $3.00 each
Spark Plug Wire Set
↳ $20.00 to $80.00 per set
Distributor Cap and Rotor
↳ $15.00 to $30.00 per set
Ignition Module
↳ $40.00 to $200.00 each
Ignition Coil
↳ $50.00 each
Coil Packs
↳ $100.00 to $200.00 per set
Battery
↳ $40.00 to $80.00 each

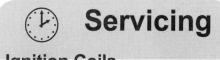

Servicing

Ignition Coils
- Change when faulty

Ignition Module

The ignition module, used on electronic and distributorless ignition systems, is basically a switch that turns the low voltage from the battery on and off to the ignition coil(s). It is a transistor that is timed and controlled by an on-board computer. In conventional ignition systems, contact points controlled system spark mechanically.

Distributor Cap and Rotor

The distributor cap and rotor (*Figure 11.5*), used on conventional and electronic ignition systems, distributes or sends high voltage to each spark plug. The rotor rotates inside the cap, connecting and sending high voltage to one terminal at a time.

Figure 11.5   **Distributor Cap and Rotor**

Servicing

Distributor Cap and Rotor
- Change every 25,000 to 50,000 miles

Trouble Guide

Engine Misses
- Faulty spark plug wires
- Worn spark plugs
- Worn distributor cap or rotor

Spark Plug Wires

Spark plug wires (*Figure 11.6*) are used on all generations of electrical systems. On the conventional and electronic ignition systems, spark plug wires connect the distributor to the spark plugs at each cylinder. In the distributorless ignition system, the spark plug wires connect the coil packs to the spark plugs. The spark plug wires carry high voltage electricity.

Figure 11.6   **Spark Plug Wires**

✓ Tech Tip

Changing Spark Plug Wires

Changing the spark plug wires is relatively easy. A couple of tips should be taken into account. Engines have certain *firing orders* that cannot be mixed up. Remove and replace only one wire at a time to avoid mixing up the wires. It is also a good practice to use dielectric grease in the boot end of each spark plug wire to inhibit corrosion.

Spark Plugs

The spark plug (*Figure 11.7*), used in all generations of ignition systems, completes the high voltage circuit. Voltage at the spark plug needs to be great enough to arc across a gap thus creating a spark. This spark is what ignites the air-fuel mixture. The center electrode on the spark plug is commonly made of copper or platinum. The gap between the center electrode and the grounded electrode is usually between 0.020 to 0.080 of an inch. Most engines have one spark plug per cylinder.

Figure 11.7   *Spark Plug*

✓ Tech Tip

Changing Spark Plugs

When changing spark plugs, it is recommended to use anti-seize compound on the threads. This prevents seizing that can result from the reaction when different metals come in contact with one another – especially important on vehicles with aluminum heads. This also allows easier removal of the spark plugs during the next service.

🕐 Servicing

Spark Plugs

- On conventional ignition systems, every 10,000 miles
- On electronic ignition systems, every 25,000 miles
- On distributorless ignition systems, every 50,000 to 75,000 miles

Crankshaft and Camshaft Sensors

The crankshaft and camshaft sensors are used on distributorless ignition systems. They keep track of piston and valve positions in the engine to efficiently time the spark.

Summary

The ignition system is designed to ignite the air-fuel mixture in the combustion chamber. Ignition systems have gone through three stages: conventional, electronic, and distributorless. Even though the ignition system may seem complex with computers, ignition modules, and sensors, there are things that the do-it-yourselfer can do to maintain and tune-up the engine to make it run smoothly for thousands of miles.

💿 CD Activities

Ignition System

- Ignition System Activity
- Chapter 11 Study Questions

CHAPTER 12

Suspension and Steering System

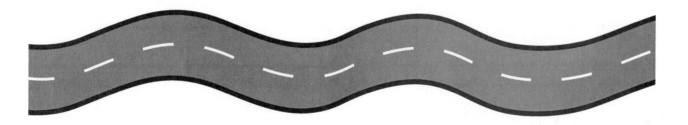

Contents

Introduction

Most of the roads that we drive on are not perfectly smooth and straight. S-curves, potholes, speed bumps (*Figure 12.1*), construction zones, and weather conditions make it necessary for vehicles to have control mechanisms. A properly working suspension and steering system gives the operator and passengers of the vehicle a smooth and pleasant ride. Shocks, struts, springs, and tires all assist in controlling the automobile by keeping the tires in contact with the road. This chapter presents the functions and components of suspension and steering systems.

Figure 12.1   *Bump Road Sign*

Objectives

Upon completion of this chapter and activities on the CD, you should be able to:
- Define the purpose of the suspension system.
- Identify the functions of suspension system components.
- Define the purpose of the steering system.
- Identify the functions of the steering system components.
- Discuss the importance of tires and explain their ratings.
- Inspect the suspension and steering components.
- Inspect and rotate tires.

🚚 Trouble Guide

Body Rolls Around Corners
- Defective shocks, struts, or springs

Purpose of the Suspension System

The suspension system helps to control the up and down movement of the vehicle. During braking or going over bumps the suspension system helps provide stability, safety, and control of the vehicle.

Suspension System Components

The suspension components consist of many parts, all of which are attached to and become a part of the chassis. The chassis consists of some or all of the following components:
- Frame or Unibody
- Shocks
- Springs
- Struts

Figure 12.2   *Coil Spring*

Frame or Unibody

The vehicle must have a foundation upon which to build the rest of the vehicle. Some vehicles have a ladder type steel frame that runs the length of the vehicle. Others have partial frames, called unibodies, that connect the body and frame into one unit.

Shocks

The shocks (*Figures 12.2 - 12.4*) on a vehicle reduce the up and down motion that is produced from going over bumps on the highway. One end of the shock absorber is connected to a stationary part on the frame or unibody, while the other is connected to a suspension component that moves. The shock absorber contains a gas, fluid, and/or compressed air to reduce the number of oscillations (up and down motions) that are produced from driving on uneven roads. Oil leakage around the shock is a sign of it needing replacement.

Figure 12.3   *Shock*

Springs

Springs work in conjunction with the shocks to help absorb the irregularities in the road surface. Springs come in coil and semi-elliptical shapes. Coil springs (*Figure 12.2*) are common on the front and rear of a number of vehicles. Semi-elliptical springs, usually called leaf springs (*Figure 12.4*), are common on the rear of trucks.

Figure 12.4   *Leaf Springs*

✓ Tech Tip

Bounce Test

To test the shocks and/or struts on a vehicle push down as hard as you can on the end that you want to test and then let go. The vehicle should come to a rest after one cycle. If it cycles more than once, the shocks, struts, or springs could be worn out.

Struts

Struts (*Figure 12.5*) have become popular on a number of vehicles. Struts basically eliminate the need for shocks and springs on the front and/or rear of a vehicle. They do this by combining the shock and spring into one unit. Struts reduce the weight and space that a comparable spring and shock would use. It should be noted that some vehicles have struts in the front and shocks and springs in the rear while others have struts at each wheel.

Figure 12.5   *Strut*

💰 Price Guide

Radial Tires
↳ $40.00 to $150.00 each
Wheel Alignments
↳ $40.00 to $80.00 labor
Tire Repairs
↳ $10.00 to $15.00 including labor
Shocks
↳ $50.00 a pair
Struts
↳ $100.00 a pair

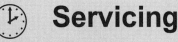

Servicing

Wheel Alignment
- When installing new tires or if a problem exists.

Purpose of the Steering System

The steering system controls the directional movements (*Figure 12.6*) of the vehicle. The steering system, in conjunction with the suspension system, provides control and stability of the vehicle. The motion the operator makes at the steering wheel is transferred to the front wheels.

Figure 12.6 *Curve Road Sign*

Steering System Components

Some of the steering system components are connected to the frame of the vehicle while others need to move with the suspension. The following are some of the basic components of the steering system:
- Steering Wheel
- Steering Linkage
- Power Steering Pump

Steering Wheel

The steering wheel (*Figure 12.7*) is how the operator controls the direction of a vehicle. Slight movements of the steering wheel can easily turn a 2000+ pound vehicle. The steering wheel is connected to the wheels by steering linkage.

Figure 12.7 *Steering Wheel*

Steering Linkage

Steering linkage connects the steering shaft from the steering wheel to the arms that control the wheels on the highway. Steering linkage can include tie rods and tie rod ends (*Figure 12.8*), steering knuckles, idler arms, center links, adjusting sleeves, and pitman arms. Many newer vehicles now incorporate a rack and pinion system that works in conjunction with a strut type suspension system to reduce space and weight. The rack, a flat piece with teeth, is connected to the tie rods. The pinion is connected to the steering shaft from the steering wheel. As the operator turns the steering wheel, the pinion turns, moving the rack in the desired direction.

Trouble Guide

Hard Steering
- Low power steering fluid
- Loose belt

Figure 12.8   *Outer Tie-Rod*

Power Steering Pump

To reduce the amount of effort that a driver needs to exert when steering, a power steering pump is commonly used. The pump, which is driven by a belt on the engine, provides fluid pressure to ease the turning force required by the operator to turn the steering wheel. It is necessary to periodically check the power steering pump reservoir fluid level.

🚑 Trouble Guide

Vehicle Pulls to One Side

- Uneven tire pressure
- Defective tire
- Out of alignment
- Brake caliper stuck

Tires

The tires (*Figure 12.9*) on a vehicle provide the connection to the road surface. The tires are part of both the steering and suspension system. They are a critical component to driving safely. Tires provide the needed traction (friction) to make driving safe during acceleration, cornering, and braking. The design of tire tread, the part of the tire that comes in contact with the road, determines how well a tire will act on different road conditions, such as ice, water, mud, and snow. A tire with very little tread is more likely to hydroplane. A tire hydroplanes when it is riding on a thin film of water. A tire with tread less than 1/16th of an inch is worn out. Tire wear indicator bars, set at 1/16th of an inch, run perpendicular to the tread to indicate when there is a need for new tires. Tires are designed to give passengers a comfortable ride and the needed traction to control the vehicle. Correct tire pressure is critical to tire wear and handling of the vehicle. Rotating tires and aligning wheels extend tire life. There is more about checking tire pressure and completing tire rotations in the activities on the attached CD. When replacing tires on a vehicle, several things should be considered:

- Tire Plies
- Tire Sizes
- Tire Grading
- Load Ratings

Figure 12.9   *Tire and Wheel Assembly*

Tire Plies

Steel belted all-season radial tires are the most common type of tire. They consist of steel wires running around the tire. Radial ply cords run from the bead (where the tire attaches to the wheel rim) on one side to the bead on the other side. In addition to this, there are other belts directly under the tread for added stability.

🚑 Trouble Guide

Vibration

- Out of balance tire
- Tire has broken belts

Tire Sizes

Tires come in a variety of sizes depending on vehicle size and weight. It is important to replace the tires on the vehicle with the size recommended by the manufacturer. Having tires too big or too small will influence how a vehicle handles. Most tires today are sized in the metric system. The following is an example tire size: *P205/70SR14*. The first letter can start with a *P*, *C*, *LT*, or *T*. *P* stands for passenger, *C* stands for commercial, *LT* stands for light truck, and *T* stands for temporary. Most cars will have passenger tires (***Figure 12.10***). Light trucks can come with either passenger or light truck type tires. The *205* stands for the tire width in millimeters. The *70* stands for the aspect ratio or profile of the tire. It compares the cross-sectional height to the cross-sectional width. A lower number will result in an overall lower, wider tire. The letter *S* may or may not be present on all tires. This indicates that the tire has been tested at speeds at or above 112 mph. Other speed rated letters are *H* (130 mph), *V* (149 mph), and *Z* (+149 mph) – each being tested at the corresponding speeds. The next letter *R* identifies that the tire is a radial type tire. The last number represents the rim diameter in inches. The tire in (***Figure 12.10***) fits a 14-inch rim. Common rim sizes are 13, 14, 15, 16, and 17-inch.

Figure 12.10   *Tire Sidewall Information*

Tire Grading

All passenger (*P*) vehicle tires will have UTQG (uniform tire quality grading) ratings that have been established by the United States Department of Transportation (DOT). These have been established to help the consumer compare tire brands and types. The three UTQG ratings (***Figure 12.11***) are treadwear, traction, and temperature.

✓ Tech Tip

Rotating Tires

Rotating tires improves tire life. Check your owner's manual for the rotation pattern. It is important to torque the lug nuts in a star pattern. Torque refers to getting all of the lug nuts to the same tightness. A torque wrench is needed to torque wheels to the correct setting. Over tightened lug nuts will make it difficult to change the tire in the future, while under tightened lug nuts may loosen up and cause the wheel to come off. In addition, unevenly tightened lug nuts can warp brake drums and rotors.

The treadwear rating, given as a number, is based on the wear rate of the tire when tested in a controlled setting. For example, a tire graded 300 will last twice as long as a 150 tire. Traction ratings, shown as *AA*, *A*, *B*, or *C*, represent a tire's ability to grip the road on a wet surface. An *AA* rating has superb traction, an *A* rating has excellent traction, a *B* rating has good traction, and a *C* rated tire has poor traction. The third rating, temperature, represents a tires ability to resist high-temperatures. These are rated as being *A*, *B*, or *C* – where *A* can withstand the highest temperature.

	Best ⟷ Poor			
Treadwear	500+			100
Traction	AA	A	B	C
Temperature	A		B	C

Figure 12.11 ***UTQG Scale***

Load Ratings

Tires are also classified by the amount of load (weight) that they can carry. Most passenger car tires are rated as either standard or extra load. Light truck tires have 4-ply (B load range), 6-ply (C load range), 8-ply (D load range), 10-ply (E load range), or a 12-ply rating (F load range). The load range, ply rating, and maximum inflation pressure are all related. The more plies a tire has, the more load it can carry.

Web Links

Suspension and Steering System Related Sites

Monroe Shocks and Struts
↳ www.monroe.com
Performance Suspension Technology
↳ www.p-s-t.com
Tenneco Automotive
↳ www.tenneco-automotive.com
TireRack.Com
↳ www.tirerack.com
National Highway Traffic Safety Administration
↳ www.nhtsa.dot.gov
Toyo Tires
↳ www.toyo.com
Goodyear Tires
↳ www.goodyear.com
Cooper Tires
↳ www.coopertires.com
Michelin Tires
↳ www.michelin.com
Kelly Springfield Tires
↳ www.kelly-springfield.com
Uniroyal Tires
↳ www.uniroyal.com
Bridgestone/Firestone Tires
↳ www.firestone.com
Rubber Manufacturers Association
↳ www.rma.org

Underinflation

Overinflation

Cupping - Worn
Components or
Out of Balance

Misalignment

Figure 12.12   *Abnormal Tire Wear*

🚑 Trouble Guide

Excessive Tire Wear

- Incorrect tire pressure
- Excessive speeds in turns
- Tires out of balance
- Suspension/steering components excessively worn
- Alignment incorrect

✓ Tech Tip

Liquid Tire Fix Sprays

Liquid sprays that are inserted into the tire valve are only recommended for temporary fixes. The liquid can corrode the inside of the rim and throw the tire off balance. After use, it is recommended that the tire be taken off the rim so the inside of the tire and rim can be dried, patched, and rebalanced.

Tire Wear Problems

Inspecting your tires on a regular basis will help you identify how they are wearing. Many things can cause abnormal tire wear (*Figure 12.12*): underinflation, overinflation, worn steering components, worn suspension components, tires out of balance, and tire misalignment.

✓ Tech Tip

Repairing Tires

A plug or a patch can be used to repair tires. A plug can be inserted without taking the tire off the rim. A patch is put over the hole on the inside of the tire. If a tire is removed from the rim the reassembled wheel should be rebalanced after making the repair. Only small holes in the tread can be repaired. Holes in the sidewall of the tire are not repairable. This is because the sidewall experiences too much stress from expansion and contraction as the tire rotates down the highway.

Summary

The suspension system absorbs the bumps in the road to give you a smooth ride. The steering system allows the operator to control the left and right motions of the vehicle. Tires provide the traction (friction) necessary to maneuver the vehicle. Knowing tire specifications can be beneficial when making decisions about new tires. Uniform tire quality grading ratings make it easier for you to compare different tires. Abnormal tire wear patterns can show possible problems with the vehicle. Suspension and steering components work in conjunction with one another to provide a safe ride.

💿 CD Activities

Suspension and Steering

- Suspension and Steering Activity
- Tire Inspection and Rotation Activity
- Changing a Spare Tire Activity
- Chapter 12 Study Questions

CHAPTER 13

Braking System

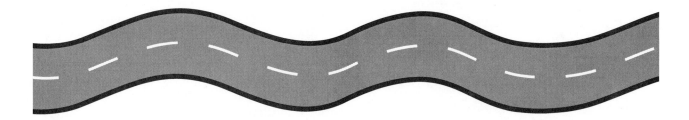

Contents

Introduction

The braking system is designed to help the operator control the deceleration of the vehicle. While the suspension and steering systems control the ride and directional movements, the braking system is designed to slow or stop the vehicle (*Figure 13.1*). The braking system is crucial to the safe operation of the vehicle. This chapter identifies brake components and the principles that assist in slowing a vehicle.

Figure 13.1   *Stop Road Sign*

Objectives

Upon completion of this chapter and activities on the CD, you should be able to:
*   Define the purpose and principles of the braking system.
*   Identify the different types of brakes and their components.
*   Identify brake fluid properties.
*   Discuss the advantage of antilock brakes.
*   Explain how the emergency brake is a secondary braking mechanism.
*   Safely perform basic inspections on the braking system.

Trouble Guide
Pedal Travels to the Floor
*   Low brake fluid
*   Brake fluid leak

Trouble Guide
Spongy Brakes
*   Air in the brake system

Purpose of the Braking System

The braking system is designed to decrease the speed of the vehicle. In order to slow the vehicle there needs to be friction between parts. Unlike the lubrication system, where minimizing friction is the goal, the braking system is designed to use friction for control. The amount of friction created needs to be controlled by the operator of the vehicle. This is done by the force the operator exerts on the brake pedal. Force is defined as the pushing or pulling action of one object upon another. In this example, the operator's foot is one object, while the brake pedal is the other object. The brake pedal is mechanically connected to a hydraulic unit called a master cylinder (*Figure 13.2*). The master cylinder is where brake fluid is stored. As force is exerted on

Figure 13.2   *Brake Master Cylinder*

the brake pedal, fluid is sent to all of the wheels through brake lines. Once at the wheels, the fluid pressure is converted back to mechanical pressure. This pressure causes the brake pads or shoes (discussed later) to move to create the needed friction against a rotating disc or drum at the wheels to slow the vehicle. Friction increases as the operator pushes harder on the brake pedal.

Types of Brakes

The two types of brakes commonly used on the automobile are:

- Disc Brakes (*Figure 13.3*)
- Drum Brakes (*Figure 13.4*)

Some vehicles only have disc brakes, but many vehicles have a combination of the two systems. On vehicles with both systems, disc brakes are usually front brakes while drum brakes are usually rear brakes. Disc and drum brake systems use a brake pedal, master cylinder, and brake lines. The major difference between the disc and drum brake systems is the hardware at the wheels. Both disc and drum brake systems use a frictional type material that slowly wears as the brakes are applied. More recently, manufacturers have been installing disc brakes on all four wheels as standard equipment.

✓ Tech Tip

Warped Brakes

If a pulsation is noticed when the brakes are applied, the rotors may be warped. Brake rotors can become warped if lug nuts are not tightened to the correct torque. The rotors can also become warped if cold water comes in contact with them immediately after the brakes have been used excessively.

Figure 13.4   **Brake Drums**

⛑ Trouble Guide

Pulsating Brakes

- Disc warped
- Drum warped

Figure 13.3   **Brake Disc (Rotor)**

Disc Brakes

The disc brake system consists of a disc, also called a rotor, connected to the wheel of the vehicle. A set of brake pads (*Figure 13.5*) hug the rotor. As force is applied to the brake pedal, the brake pads hug the rotor tighter causing more friction. The friction causes the vehicle to slow down. A caliper converts the fluid pressure in the brake lines to the mechanical motion of the pads.

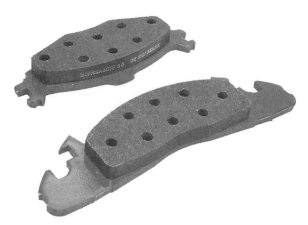

Figure 13.5   **Brake Pads**

Figure 13.6   **Brake Shoes**

Drum Brakes

The drum brake system consists of a drum that is connected to the wheel. Inside the drum is a set of brake shoes (*Figure 13.6*). As a force is applied to the brake pedal, the brake shoes are forced out causing friction with the drum. This friction causes the vehicle to slow down. A wheel cylinder (*Figure 13.7*) converts the fluid pressure in the brake lines to mechanical motion of the shoes.

Figure 13.7   **Wheel Cylinder**

Servicing

Brake Fluid
- Change every 4 years, 48,000 miles, or during brake service

Brake Fluid

Brake fluid links major braking system components. Brake fluid travels through lines to connect the master cylinder to the calipers in a disc brake system or wheel cylinders in a drum brake system. Brake fluid must be able to flow freely at high and low temperatures. Brake fluid absorbs water and thus should always be kept in sealed containers. Brake fluid fights corrosion, lubricates moving parts, and protects metal, plastic, and rubber components. The most common type of brake fluid is DOT 3, but always refer to the owner's manual for the specific vehicle. *Warning: If brake fluid is spilled on a vehicle's finish, it will strip paint.*

Antilock Brakes

Antilock brakes can be used with both disc and drum brake systems. In a conventional braking system, the wheels are likely to lockup if the operator applies a large enough force to the brake pedal. During wheel lockup, the operator's braking distance increases and control of steering decreases. Antilock brake systems reduce

Price Guide

Brake Fluid
↳ $1.00 to $3.00 a pint
Brake Pads
↳ $30.00 to $50.00 a set (parts)
Brake Shoes
↳ $15.00 to $30.00 a set (parts)
Brake Rotor or Drum
↳ $50.00 each (parts)

✓ Tech Tip

Air in the Brake System

Often when brake components are replaced, air gets into the system. Air, unlike brake fluid, is compressible. When air gets into the system the operator will notice a very spongy and soft brake pedal. If this happens, the system must be bled. Bleeding the air out of the system consists of pushing the air out of a "bleeder" at the caliper or wheel cylinder.

wheel lockup. Antilock systems use sensors and computers to monitor wheel speed. If a sensor notices that a wheel is about to lockup, it releases pressure in the caliper or wheel cylinder. Antilock brake systems (ABS) help the vehicle stop faster and the operator maintain control. Some automobiles have antilock brakes on two wheels, while others have antilock brakes on all four wheels. If a vehicle only has two-wheel antilock brakes, the antilock brake system is usually in the rear of the vehicle.

Emergency Brakes

Emergency (parking) brakes use the same hardware at the wheels to stop the vehicle, but use a different connection mechanism. Instead of using fluid as the connection between the pedal and the brakes, it uses a mechanical cable. This allows one system to work independently of the other. If the vehicle unexpectedly loses brake fluid, the emergency brake would still work. However, the emergency brake only connects to the rear brakes, so braking distance will greatly increase.

Web Links

Brake System Related Sites

Raybestos Brakes
↳ www.raybestos.com

Federal-Mogul (Wagner Brake Products)
↳ www.federal-mogul.com

Bendix Brakes
↳ www.bendixbrakes.com

Midas International Corporation
↳ www.midas.com

Meineke Muffler and Brake
↳ www.meineke.com

Summary

Brake systems use friction to slow and stop a vehicle. The two types of brake systems used today are disc and drum brakes. Disc brakes use rotors, pads, and calipers. Drum brakes use drums, shoes, and wheel cylinders. Antilock brakes assist in preventing wheel lockup and provide the operator with maximum directional control. The parking brake uses a mechanical linkage (cable) instead of a fluid linkage (brake fluid) as a secondary stopping method in emergencies.

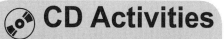 CD Activities

Braking System

- Brake Inspection Activity
- Chapter 13 Study Questions

CHAPTER 14

Drivetrains

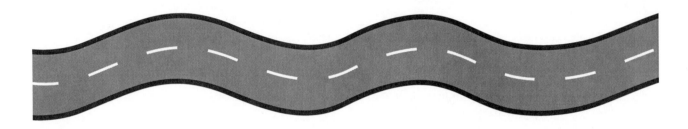

Contents

Introduction

Objectives

Purpose of the Drivetrain

Drivetrain Components

Drivetrain Systems

Summary

Introduction

The engine can provide all the power in the world, but if it isn't transferred to the wheels the car will not move. Automobiles need to perform equally well under a variety of loads. The transfer of power needs to accommodate the conditions on the highway, the weight of the vehicle and its passengers, and the performance desired to accelerate. Today's automobile buyers can choose between rear-wheel, front-wheel, four-wheel, or all-wheel drivetrains. This chapter discusses the purpose of the drivetrain, drivetrain components, and types of drivetrains.

Objectives

Upon completion of this chapter and activities on the CD, you should be able to:
- Define the purpose of the drivetrain.
- Identify drivetrain components.
- Identify and describe different drivetrain systems.
- Inspect drivetrain systems.

🚑 Trouble Guide

Automatic Transmission Slips Constantly Shifting from One Gear to Another
- Low Fluid
- Worn Transmission

Purpose of the Drivetrain

The purpose of the drivetrain (*Figure 14.1*) is to transfer power from the engine to the wheels in order to propel the vehicle. This transfer needs to be done smoothly and efficiently. Without smooth transitions, the automobile would not be very comfortable or easy to drive. The drivetrain also helps to control the speed and power through gears.

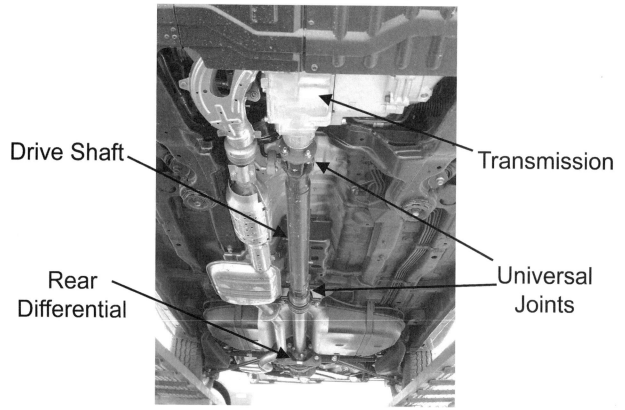

Drive Shaft

Transmission

Rear Differential

Universal Joints

Figure 14.1   *Drivetrain Components on a Rear-Wheel Drive Vehicle*

Checking Transmission Fluid

The fluid level on most automatic transmissions is checked with a dipstick. Most manufacturers require that the engine be running while in park or neutral. The most common automatic transmission fluid is Dexron/Mercon®. New automatic transmission fluid is a pinkish color. Manual transmissions have a different checking method. A plug on the side of the transmission housing is used to check manual transmission fluid levels. Some manual transmissions actually take automatic transmission fluid, while others use 80W90 gear oil. When servicing or adding fluid to a transmission, always check the owner's manual.

Drivetrain Components

Several components need to work together to transfer the power smoothly and efficiently from the engine to the wheels:

- Gears
- Transmissions
- Drive shafts
- Clutches

Gears

Gears are used in power transfer systems. Gears are always in sets. Gears can be used to change speed, torque, and direction of travel.

Difficult to Shift Gears in a Manual Transmission

- Worn Clutch
- Faulty Clutch Slave Cylinder
- Air in Hydraulic Clutch System

Manual Transmission Fluid

- Change according to owner's manual

Figure 14.2   *Manual Transmission*

Transmissions

Gears are housed in a transmission. A transmission can be automatic, manual (*Figure 14.2*), or constant variable. In automatic transmissions the gear shifting is done automatically. All the operator has to select is the forward or reverse gear. Many transmissions today are computer controlled electronic transmissions that calculate the most efficient time to shift. In manual transmissions the operator of the vehicle does the gear shifting manually. Manual transmissions commonly come in 3, 4, or 5 speeds. Constant variable transmissions have recently begun to appear on some passenger cars. Instead of using gears they use two variable speed cone-shaped pulleys in conjunction with a belt. Transmissions change the power to the wheels for different applications. Maintaining a steady speed requires less power than accelerating to that speed.

Automatic Transmission Fluid (ATF) and Filter

- Change every 2 years, 24,000 miles, or as recommended by the manufacturer

Figure 14.4   ***Standard Drive Shaft***

have a combination of constant velocity (CV) and standard drive shafts. Standard drive shafts have joints, called universal or U-joints (*Figures 14.5 and 14.6*), to accept the moving chassis. The shafts, whatever the type, are designed to transfer power from the transmission to the wheels.

Drive Shafts

On front-wheel drive vehicles two drive shafts, called constant velocity (CV) shafts (*Figure 14.3*), connect the transmission to the wheels. On rear-wheel drive vehicles, the drive shaft (*Figure 14.4*) connects the transmission to the rear differential, which sends the power to the wheels. Four-wheel and all-wheel drive vehicles usually

Figure 14.5   ***U-Joint***

Figure 14.3   ***Constant Velocity Shaft***

Figure 14.6   **Installed U-Joint**

💰 Price Guide

Automatic Transmission Fluid
↳ $1.00 to $2.00 a quart
CV Joint
↳ $75.00 to $125.00 each (parts)
U-Joint
↳ $10.00 to $20.00 each (parts)
Clutch and Pressure Plate
↳ $100.00 to $300.00 (parts)

Clutches

A clutch disc is used in conjunction with a pressure plate (*Figure 14.7*) in a manual transmission to shift gears. The clutch is the connection between the transmission and engine. When the clutch is engaged, the engine is driving the transmission. When the clutch is disengaged (when the clutch pedal is depressed), the transmission is disconnected from the rotational motion of the engine's crankshaft. A pressure plate works in conjunction with the clutch disc to aid in the engaging and disengaging process. This allows the operator the ability to shift from one gear to the next.

Drivetrain Systems

Drivetrain systems can be divided into the following categories:
- Rear-Wheel Drive
- Front-Wheel Drive
- Four-Wheel Drive
- All-Wheel Drive

Rear-Wheel Drive

On a rear-wheel drive vehicle the power from the transmission is transferred to the rear wheels. This was the standard on cars before the 1980s. This has been and still is the standard on most pickups.

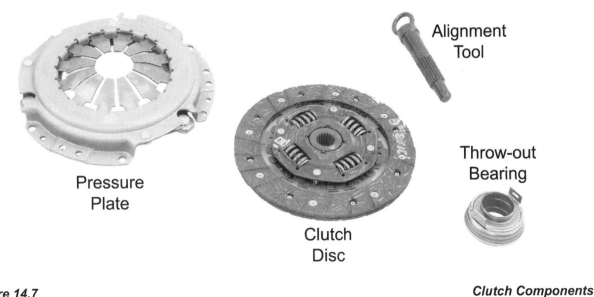

Alignment
Tool

Throw-out
Bearing

Pressure
Plate

Clutch
Disc

Figure 14.7   **Clutch Components**

Front-Wheel Drive

On a front-wheel drive vehicle the power from the transmission is transferred to the front wheels. This is the standard on most cars today. The weight of the engine on the front wheels gives front-wheel drive cars extremely good traction on diverse road conditions.

Four-Wheel Drive

On a four-wheel drive vehicle the power from the transmission is transferred to the rear and/or front wheels. On most four-wheel drive vehicles the operator has the choice of selecting either two-wheel drive or four-wheel drive. Many trucks have this option. Four-wheel drive vehicles have a tendency to get worse gas mileage than two-wheel drive vehicles. This is from the addition of friction from the drivetrain turning more components.

Web Links

Drivetrain Related Sites

Qualitee International (Clutch Kits)
↳ www.qualitee.com
Brute Power Clutch Kits
↳ www.brutepower.com
AutoZone Automotive Parts
↳ www.autozone.com
Federated Auto Parts
↳ www.federatedautoparts.com

All-Wheel Drive

On an all-wheel drive vehicle the power from the transmission is transferred to the front wheels and rear wheels. All-wheel drive systems are different from four-wheel drive systems. The operator doesn't have the control to select from two-wheel drive to four-wheel drive. All-wheel drive vehicles use electronics to control the power transfer to the wheels. Speed sensors are mounted on each wheel to monitor wheel traction. Under normal conditions the vehicle is two-wheel drive. The benefit of an all-wheel drive vehicle is that when traction is lost at any one wheel, the power is transferred to another. The result is superior traction and control. More and more automotive manufacturers are using all-wheel drivetrain systems on a broad range of vehicles.

Summary

Drivetrains transfer power from the engine to the wheels. Gears, transmissions, and drive shafts are used to transmit the power efficiently. Vehicles can be front-, rear-, four-, or all-wheel drive. All-wheel drive vehicles have become popular because they have superior traction on all types of road conditions.

CD Activities

Drivetrain

- Drivetrain Activity
- Chapter 14 Study Questions

CHAPTER 15

Exhaust and Emissions

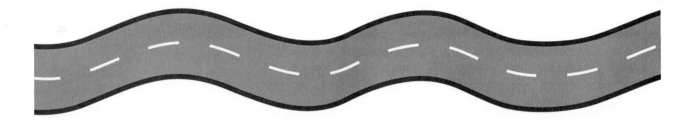

Contents

Introduction

Exhaust and emission systems on newer vehicles have become more complex than in the past. The emission system is used to monitor air-fuel ratios and has many benefits to the operator and the environment. For many years, automotive manufacturers were just concerned about getting the hot exhaust gases out to the side or rear of the vehicle. Today exhaust and emission systems are complex mechanisms that provide safety, efficiency, and concern for our fragile environment. Periodically, exhaust and emission system components need replacing. This chapter focuses on identifying the components and purposes of the exhaust and emission system.

Objectives

Upon completion of this chapter and activities on the CD, you should be able to:
- Define the purpose of the exhaust and emission system.
- Identify and explain the components in an exhaust and emission system.
- Inspect exhaust and emission system components.

Purpose of the Exhaust and Emission System

Exhaust and emission systems are designed to deal with the inefficient by-products of the internal combustion process. The exhaust system is designed to dampen the sound of the engine. The emission system is designed to lower the pollution of the vehicle.

Servicing

Exhaust
- Inspect once a year
- Change as needed

Exhaust Components

The exhaust system consists of the following components:
- Exhaust Manifolds
- Exhaust Pipes
- Muffler
- Hangers and Clamps

Exhaust Manifolds

The exhaust manifolds, usually made out of cast iron, connect directly to the engine. The exhaust manifolds are designed to harness the exhaust gases from the numerous cylinders into one pipe. Inline engines have one exhaust manifold, while V-engines have two (one for each bank of cylinders).

Exhaust Pipes

Exhaust pipes are tubes of steel that connect other components such as the exhaust manifolds to the catalytic converter. An exhaust pipe also connects the catalytic converter to the muffler. This pipe is called the intermediate pipe. Another pipe, a tail pipe (*Figure 15.1*), expels the exhaust from the muffler.

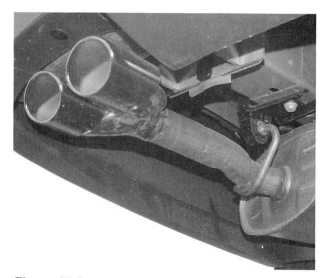

Figure 15.1   *Tail Pipe*

🚑 Trouble Guide

Excessively Loud

- Hole in muffler
- Hole in exhaust pipes
- Worn exhaust manifold gaskets

Muffler

The muffler (*Figure 15.2*), usually oval or cylindrical in shape, is used to deaden the sound from the engine. It is basically a silencer to aid in the reduction of noise pollution and is located after the catalytic converter, but before the tail pipe.

Figure 15.2   *Muffler*

✓ **Tech Tip**

Replacing Exhaust Components

Often the muffler on the exhaust system rusts out before anything else. This is because water vapor has a tendency to collect in the muffler. Most factory exhaust systems are welded assemblies from the catalytic to the tail pipe. It is relatively easy to replace everything from the catalytic on back, even if the muffler is the only worn out part. If you have a shop replace only the muffler, it may cost about as much as if you replaced the system from the catalytic on back. If you just replace the muffler there is usually a lot of cutting and fabricating, which equates to more labor. Replacing all the components from the catalytic on back is usually just a matter of bolting and hanging the parts in place.

Hangers and Clamps

Exhaust hangers (*Figure 15.3*) suspend the whole exhaust system. The hanger must allow some flexibility. The exhaust is connected to the engine and to the body. As the engine runs, it vibrates. If the exhaust system was connected solidly to the body, stress cracks would develop. The hangers

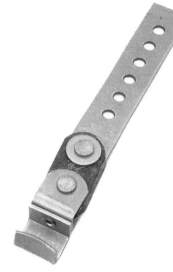

Figure 15.3   *Exhaust Hanger*

have tough rubber components to allow for flexing and vibrating. The exhaust clamps (*Figure 15.4*) connect the exhaust pipes to the muffler and catalytic converter. Exhaust clamps are usually a type of U-bolt. On new exhaust systems, welds instead of clamps hold the exhaust pipes to the muffler and the catalytic converter.

Figure 15.4   *Exhaust Clamp*

🚑 Trouble Guide

Engine Running Rich, Stalls, or Lacks Power

- Emission system malfunctioning

Emission Components

The environment has become a big concern for many people, and rightfully so. Vehicles produce a large amount of by-products that are harmful to our ecosystem. Consumers can minimize pollution by driving more efficient vehicles and by driving less. Planning trips will save petroleum, money, and harmful environmental effects. Emission system components presented are:

- Catalytic Converter
- Positive Crankcase Ventilation (PCV)
- Exhaust Gas Recirculation (EGR)
- Charcoal Canister
- Oxygen Sensors

✓ Tech Tip

Need the Catalytic?

People sometimes say, "Just take the catalytic converter off. It is just plugging up the rest of the system." This is highly discouraged. Automobile engines today need a properly working catalytic converter to run efficiently. In addition, it is illegal to disconnect emission system components. The computer in the automobile receives information from a number of sensors. If the catalytic or other emission system component is disconnected, the computer will run the engine either too lean or too rich. Either way, efficiency and engine life will be less. Equally as important, think of the environment.

Catalytic Converter

The catalytic converter (*Figure 15.5*) is placed under the automobile in the exhaust system between the exhaust manifold(s) and muffler. It contains a catalyst that promotes the chemical change of carbon monoxide, hydrocarbons, and nitrogen oxides into water vapor, carbon dioxide, nitrogen, and oxygen. Carbon monoxide is a poisonous chemical. Nitrogen oxide is the principle component that causes smog.

Figure 15.5   *Catalytic Converter*

PCV

The positive crankcase ventilation (PCV) system is designed to remove the effects of blow-by. As the engine runs, some unburned fuel and water vapor get past the cylinders and into the crankcase. Water can turn oil into sludge, while unburned fuel can dilute the oil. If not taken care of, water and unburned fuel can cause corrosion and increase engine wear. The PCV system recirculates the water vapor and unburned fuel back into the intake. This process will eventually burn the components in the combustion process. In the PCV system is a PCV valve that needs servicing at regular intervals. The PCV valve is commonly found between the cylinder head valve cover and the air cleaner. It is usually in a tube or connected directly into the valve cover.

🕐 Servicing

PCV Valve

- Change every 2 years, 24,000 miles, or as recommended by the manufacturer

💰 Price Guide

Muffler
↳ $20.00 to $40.00 each (parts)
Exhaust Pipes
↳ $20.00 to $40.00 each (parts)
Oxygen Sensor
↳ $30.00 to $60.00 each (parts)
Catalytic Converter
↳ $150.00 to $300.00 each (parts)

EGR

The exhaust gas recirculation system reduces nitrogen oxide emissions by diluting the air-fuel mixture with the exhaust gases. Most EGR systems have an EGR valve that is operated by a vacuum from the engine. The EGR valve regulates the amount of exhaust gases that are directed to the intake system. The EGR valve is typically mounted on the intake manifold on top of the engine.

🖱 Web Links

Exhaust and Emission Related Sites

Walker Exhaust Systems
↳ www.walkerexhaust.com
Nickson Industries (Exhaust Accessories)
↳ www.nickson.com
J.C. Whitney Inc.
↳ www.jcwhitney.com
Gibson Performance Exhaust Systems
↳ www.gibsonperformance.com
Arvin Industries (Exhaust Systems)
↳ www.arvin.com
Tenneco Automotive
↳ www.tenneco-automotive.com
Tomco Inc.
↳ www.tomco-inc.com
Dynomax Exhaust
↳ www.dynomax.com

🕐 Servicing

Carbon Canister Filter

• As recommended by the manufacturer

Charcoal Canister

A charcoal canister is put into the emission system to lower the release of hydrocarbons into the air. On many vehicles it looks like a coffee can and is located under the hood.

Oxygen Sensors

Oxygen sensors (*Figure 15.6*) are usually placed before and/or after the catalytic converter. The oxygen sensor monitors the oxygen content in the vehicle's exhaust. It sends signals to the computer to maintain a 14.7 to 1 (the best) air to fuel ratio. This ratio of air to fuel makes the engine run smooth, efficient, and in the end, pollute less.

Figure 15.6   *Oxygen Sensor*

Summary

As technology advances, the internal combustion engine will become more efficient and pollute less. Over time, components have been added to vehicles to lower noise and reduce chemical pollution. The exhaust system reduces noise, while the emission control system converts harmful gases into more environmentally friendly by-products.

💿 CD Activities

Exhaust and Emissions

• Exhaust and Emissions Activity
• Chapter 15 Study Questions

Index

Here's the Buzz on Auto Upkeep

"If you have a new driver in the family, we suggest you invest in a copy of *Auto Upkeep: Basic Car Care* by Michael Gray. It's a straightforward, well-written primer on all aspects of automotive design and maintenance. Mr. Gray covers everything from washing to brake wear. It's all broken down into easy to understand chapters, each covering a major system. There's even a CD with a well-designed study guide included in every copy. Experienced gear heads will find it to be somewhat simplistic, but for a raw beginner, this is an absolute must-read."

John Davis, Host of *MotorWeek*, Television's Original Automotive Magazine

"If you own a vehicle, want to buy a vehicle or ever intend to do your own maintenance, please read this book first. If you have ever considered working on automobiles for a living or even as a hobby, I strongly recommend this text. It is written in a down to earth, easy to understand manner with excellent graphics and explanations. Take it from me: Don't touch your car without consulting this book."

Jerry R. Johnson, Assistant Professor of Automotive Technology at Salt Lake Community College
Director of The Digital Automotive Education Company and AutoGlossary.com

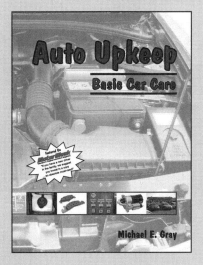

"*Auto Upkeep: Basic Car Care* by automotive expert Michael E. Gray is a practical and straightforward guide for anyone who owns a car or is considering buying one. *Auto Upkeep* is an excellent and very highly recommended primer and self-teaching tool which is enhanced with an accompanying CD-ROM containing activities, website links, and study questions."

MidWest Book Review

"What a novice idea! Someone finally wrote a book that I can use in a beginning automotive class! I've taught for 30 years+ and have never seen an automotive book that doesn't intimidate students. They actually like this one and enjoy reading about cars. I would highly recommend this book for students of automotive classes and for the novice out there!"

Automotive Teacher

"*Auto Upkeep: Basic Car Care* by Michael E. Gray - Originally written for an automotive consumer course, this book walks students (and adults) through the fundamentals of car ownership: buying a car, choosing insurance, safely working around and on an automobile, paying expenses, and doing preventive maintenance and basic repair. Comprehensive, yet easy to read, the guide also includes a CD-ROM with activities for students and study questions."

From *NEA Today* - The Magazine of the National Education Association
May 2004, Page 59, Volume 22, Number 8

"This is one book that explains important areas of car care in a way that won't overwhelm an average individual. Anyone could benefit from owning this book and it could be a second owner's manual for many. The tech tips are quick and useful as a reference. I have reviewed other books, but this one is by far, I feel, the easiest for the basic consumer to comprehend."

Al Starrine, Assistant Professor, Automotive Service Technology, Northern Michigan University

See Other Side for Order Information

Auto Upkeep: Basic Car Care

About the Book

Auto Upkeep: Basic Car Care is an introductory book providing individuals with the knowledge to make economical decisions and take preventative measures to enhance the overall satisfaction of being an automotive consumer. Each chapter includes helpful guides regarding servicing, tech tips, troubleshooting, calculations, average prices, and web links. The accompanying CD contains text study questions and activity procedures. Chapter tests and teacher keys are available upon request for instructors.

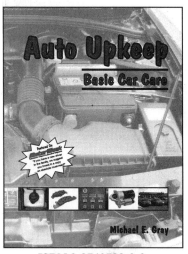

ISBN 0-9740792-0-0
Trade Paperback

Quantity Discounts

Discounts are available for educational institutions, libraries, and fund-raising when purchasing multiple copies. Purchase orders are accepted.

Order Direct from the Publisher

To order *Auto Upkeep: Basic Car Care* visit:

www.rollinghillspublishing.com

Rolling Hills Publishing

P.O. Box 724
New Windsor, MD 21776

CD Activities

Chapter 1: Identify VIN, make, model, year, type, and engine size.

Chapter 2: Research buying a car, MSRP, dealer invoice, and dealer cost.

Chapter 3: Calculate loan payment, sales tax, license, registration, fuel, insurance, maintenance, and unexpected repairs.

Chapter 4: Identify and become familiar with emergency and safety equipment.

Chapter 5: Wash the exterior, clean the interior, and wax the finish.

Chapter 6: Check the fluid levels in various components.

Chapter 7: Clean and test a battery. Test the alternator. Jump start a vehicle. Replace various lights on a vehicle. Test the starter.

Chapter 8: Change the oil and filter.

Chapter 9: Identify components of the fuel system. Change the air filter, CCV filter, PCV valve, vapor canister filter, and fuel filter.

Chapter 10: Test, inspect, and service the cooling system. Test the thermostat.

Chapter 11: Install spark plugs. Inspect, test, and install spark plug wires. Inspect and install distributor cap and rotor.

Chapter 12: Change a spare tire. Inspect and perform basic service procedures on suspension and steering components. Inspect tires and perform tire rotation.

Chapter 13: Inspect the disc brakes.

Chapter 14: Inspect the drivetrain components.

Chapter 15: Inspect the exhaust and emission components.

See Other Side for Reviews